Standard
GRADING GUIDE
for
CANADIAN and COLONIAL
DECIMAL COINS

by
JAMES E. CHARLTON
and
ROBERT C. WILLEY

© Copyright 1965 Whitman Publishing Company
© Copyright 1999 The Unitrade Press

Printed and Bound in Canada

ISBN 1-895909-68-6

Editorial Committee
Patrick Glassford and Bill Boynton

THE UNITRADE PRESS

99 FLORAL PARKWAY, TORONTO, ON   M6L 2C4

CONTENTS

INTRODUCTION 5

CANADA

CENTS
    Large Cents 11
    Small Cents 21

FIVE CENTS
    Silver Five Cents 29
    Nickel, Tombac and Steel Five Cents 36
    Steel, Nickel and Cupro-Nickel Five Cents 44

TEN CENTS
    Silver Ten Cents 48
    Silver and Nickel Ten Cents 59

TWENTY AND TWENTY-FIVE CENTS
    Silver Twenty and Twenty-Five Cents 61
    Silver and Nickel Twenty-Five Cents 77

FIFTY CENTS
    Silver Fifty Cents 82
    Silver and Nickel Fifty Cents 94

DOLLARS
    Silver Dollars 97
    Nickel Dollars 110
    Aureate Bronze Dollars 114

TWO DOLLARS
    Bi-Metallic Two Dollars 118

FIVE AND TEN DOLLARS
    Gold Five and Ten Dollars 119

SOVEREIGNS
    Gold Sovereigns 121

COLONIAL DECIMAL COINS – See Page Following.

COLONIAL DECIMAL COINS

NEW BRUNSWICK
Half Cents 125
Cents 127
Silver Five Cents 130
Silver Ten Cents 132
Silver Twenty Cents 134

NEWFOUNDLAND
Large Cents 137
Small Cents 144
Silver Five Cents 146
Silver Ten Cents 155
Silver Twenty Cents 164
Silver Twenty-Five Cents 171
Silver Fifty Cents 173
Gold Two Dollars 180

NOVA SCOTIA
Half Cents 183
Large Cents 185

PRINCE EDWARD ISLAND
Large Cent 188

INTRODUCTION
CHARACTERISTICS OF THE VARIOUS
CANADIAN COINAGES
Queen Victoria

The Canadian coinages of Queen Victoria were all designed by Leonard Charles Wyon and show the typical high standards of his productions. The relief is generally high and there is an almost photographic reproduction of all the details of each design. Unfortunately, there are some periods during Victoria's reign from which it is rather difficult to find coins grading VF or better because of a problem common to early Canadian coins. It was at times necessary to make a die slightly concave or convex to obtain a proper impression from it. The surfaces of the coins, as a result, curve oppositely to those of the dies.

The obverses of cents from 1859 are convex, while reverses from 1892–1901 are convex. The result is that the convex sides wear faster in circulation. Five cent and ten cent pieces are generally flat and the 1858 twenty cent piece has a slightly convex reverse. The twenty-five and fifty cent pieces exhibit convexity on coins from some years, though not to the degree of the cents. Some twenty-five cent pieces from the 1880s and most Victorian fifty cent pieces have concave reverses. Many of the early Newfoundland coins and the cents of the Maritime provinces have convex reverses. Newfoundland fifty cent pieces from 1894 to 1900 have concave reverses.

Such inequalities of striking present peculiar problems in grading and render coins in the better grades scarce. In sale catalogues, a coin with sides which grade differently is usually described by the grade of the obverse followed by the grade of the reverse, the two being separated by an oblique stroke, as VF-20/EF-40 for example.

The average condition of Victorian coins reflects to some extent the economic situation of the day. The cent, the five cent piece and the twenty-five cent piece are most often found in the better grades. These were most often saved as keepsakes and souvenirs or given as awards to children. The twenty cent piece was saved as a curio after its replacement by the twenty-five cent piece. Ten cent pieces, being useful coins, were not generally saved and therefore are not as plentiful in VF-20 or better. These were needed in ordinary commerce and were widely circulated. The fifty cent piece is also scarce in higher grades. In those days, fifty cents was too much money to put away for art's sake, being a day's wages for far too many Canadians to permit such luxury. In Newfoundland, however, the fifty cent pieces were hoarded in large numbers because the failure of the banks in 1894 caused a great distrust of paper money on the part of the people, who therefore put all their savings into silver and gold coins, which were then concealed in their homes.

King Edward VII

Edwardian issues carried on the Victorian traditions or high relief and accurate reproduction of minute details and were designed by G.W. DeSaulles. During this reign, marked examples of concavity and convexity developed. Edwardian cents have convex reverses until 1907, while the five, ten and twenty-five pieces have markedly concave reverses until and including 1905. Fifty cent pieces had slightly convex reverses in 1902 and 1903 and concave reverses in 1904 and 1905. Silver coins from 1906 and cents from 1908 are flat.

King George V

George V issues were struck in the same style as previously, with fine, clear details and generally high relief. Several important changes were made during this reign. The cent was reduced in size in 1920 and the silver five cent piece was replaced by a nickel coin of more convenient size. Silver dollars were introduced in 1935. The silver dollar is a significant coin in that it introduced a new style of workmanship involving a lower relief and a lack of minor detail, resulting in a bold, modernistic design pleasing in its simplicity. Five and ten dollar gold pieces were coined from 1912 to 1914.

The concavity problem occurs during this reign, chiefly in the silver five and ten cent pieces, the reverses of which are convex in nearly every year. Twenty-five and fifty cent pieces have convex reverses after 1921. The five and ten dollar gold pieces are slightly convex. The small cent, nickel five cent and silver dollar pieces are flat.

5

King George VI

The year 1937, the first year of the coinage of George VI, is very significant in that the old Wyon tradition of high relief and minute detail was left behind. New reverse designs were introduced for all denominations, all in the simplistic style of the silver dollar.

The five cent piece underwent various changes in shape and composition during the reign. When nickel was needed for the war effort, the composition of the five cent piece was changed to a brass alloy called "tombac" in 1942. Because tombac coins quickly tarnish to a bronze-like tone, the shape of the coin was made twelve-sided to avoid confusion with the cent. A victory design showing a lighted torch superimposed on a large V was used on five cent reverses from 1943 to 1945. The first of these issues, 1943, was also struck in tombac, but the composition was changed to chromium-plated steel for 1944 and 1945. In 1946 the nickel content was reinstated and the beaver reverse returned. The twelve-sided shape, however, continued until 1962. The five cent pieces of 1963 and 1964 were round. A commemorative five cent piece was issued in 1951 to celebrate the bicentennial of the isolation and naming of the element Nickel.

No silver dollars were produced from 1940 to 1944 during the Second World War. There were two commemorative dollar issues during the reign, in 1939 for the Royal Visit and in 1949 to commemorate Newfoundland's entry into Confederation.

All the coins of this reign are flat.

Queen Elizabeth II

Mary Gillick Obverse

The coins of Elizabeth II can be divided into three periods, each bearing a different obverse effigy. The first period (1953–1964) features a draped, laureate, youthful effigy of the Queen. The coins are in similar style to those of George VI, but the relief is, in some cases, considerably lower, resulting in a rapid deterioration of the coins during circulation. This became evident in 1953, the first year of issue, when it was necessary to retouch the obverse die. The leaves of the wreath were cut a little more deeply and the details of the drapery over the shoulder were more strongly engraved. Because of the recutting of the lines of the drapery, coins struck using the early and retouched dies have become known as the "no shoulder strap" and "shoulder strap" varieties.

The convexity problem occurred again on fifty cent pieces from 1959 to 1963. The obverse is convex which, combined with the generally low relief, will make it difficult in the future to obtain specimens in grades higher than VF-20 unless sufficient coins were saved by dealers and investors. Other coins of this period are flat.

Commemorative silver dollars were produced in 1958 for the centenary of the establishment of British Columbia as a British Crown Colony and in 1964 for the centenary of the meetings at Charlottetown and Quebec City which led to Confederation.

Arnold Machin Obverse

The second period (1965–1989) features a more mature, draped effigy of the Queen wearing a tiara. This period in Canadian numismatics is important because of the great number of changes to our coins which occurred and the many commemorative coins struck during the twenty-five year span. The first obverse die used for the 1965 cent was flat, with small rim beads. The die proved to have a short life and was replaced by a new die which produced a concave obverse with large rim beads. Because the rim details deteriorated too rapidly, the obverse die was again changed during 1966 to produce a less concave obverse with small rim beads. The first silver dollars of 1965 have a flat obverse field and small rim beads. The flat die was retired because of its short life and a test die was introduced which produced coins with a slightly concave obverse field, medium rim beads and minor alterations to the device, notably a very fine support to the rearmost jewel of the tiara. The test die proved that concave fields would add sufficiently to the die life, so a matrix, punches and dies were prepared. Coins from these dies have a concave obverse field and even, large rim beads. Trial production runs of the 1967 dollar were made in 1966 using flat reverse dies. The coins did not strike up well and most were melted down. The replacement dies produced concave fields.

The cent was changed from round to twelve-sided from 1982 to 1996, while the five-cent piece remained basically unchanged throughout the period. During 1967, the composition of

6

the ten and twenty-five cent pieces changed from .800 to .500 silver and during the following year, 1968, the composition of both was changed to nickel. Both denominations retained their previous size and shape. The fifty cent and dollar denominations were dramatically reduced in size in 1968, from which time both were struck in nickel. The dollar underwent a further transformation with the 1987 issue when its size was further reduced, its shape was changed to eleven-sided and its composition became nickel, plated with aureate bronze. A new reverse design, featuring a loon, was also introduced at this time.

Canada's Centennial year, 1967, was celebrated by featuring a different animal or bird design by Alex Colville on the reverse of each denomination. In 1973, the reverse of the twenty-five cent piece displayed a mounted flag bearer to celebrate the centennial of the RCMP. The nickel dollars of 1970, 1971, 1973 and 1974 bore special reverse designs to celebrate the centennials of Manitoba, British Columbia, Prince Edward Island and the City of Winnipeg respectively. As well, nickel dollars bore special reverse designs for the Canadian Constitution in 1982 and in 1984 to commemorate Jacques Cartier's landing at Gaspé in 1534. A voyageur dollar was also circulated in 1982 and 1984.

Dora de Pédery-HUNT Obverse

The third period, from 1990 to date, features a contemporary, draped effigy of the Queen wearing a large diadem, necklace and earring. The reverse devices remained the same as those of the previous period. Most modern coins have been struck using slightly convex dies which produce concave fields on the coins. Time has shown that such dies strike fuller and that their imparted design elements wear more slowly, being better protected by the rim than those on coins with flat or convex fields.

The cent retained its composition and twelve-sided shape from 1990 to 1996. In 1997 the composition was changed to copper-plated zinc and the cent again became round in shape. The five, ten, twenty-five and fifty cent pieces remained basically unchanged throughout this period, except for 1992, when the coins of all denominations bore the double date 1867–1992 to celebrate the 125th anniversary of Confederation. In 1992 there were twelve different twenty-five cent pieces minted. In each case the obverse is the same and displays a slightly reduced effigy with CANADA above and the double date 1867–1992 below. Each of the twelve reverses features a different design to represent the ten provinces and two territories. In 1992, 1994 and 1995 two aureate dollars were circulated; one with the common loon reverse the other with a commemorative reverse. In 1992 the reverse featured children with a flag before the centre block of the Parliament Buildings in Ottawa. The reverses in 1994 and 1995 featured the National War Memorial and the Peacekeeping Monument respectively. No aureate dollars were minted for circulation in 1997 or 1998 and no twenty-five cent pieces were minted for circulation in 1997.

In 1996, when the two dollar note ceased production, a new two dollar coin was introduced. It is a circular bi-metallic coin, with a gold-coloured aluminum-bronze centre within a nickel outer ring. The centre of the reverse features a polar bear.

THE NEED FOR A
STANDARD GRADING SYSTEM

Whenever a coin is sold or traded there is a need for a uniform method of establishing the degree of wear it has received since it was struck. A scale for grading the amount of wear on Canadian coins has long been established and most catalogues provide a brief description, or an illustration, to explain the amount of wear for each grade. The first edition of this reference was printed in 1965 and satisfied the need, at that time, for a more thorough reference for grading each specific type of Canadian coin. It was only a few short years after the first edition was available that all the circulating coins of Canada, with the possible exception of the five-cent piece, underwent dramatic changes in their size, composition and, in some cases, their shape. Now, more than thirty years later, the first edition is still in demand even though it has been outdated, and out of print, for many years.

Contrary to the popular belief that the grading scale for Canadian coins has changed over the years, the same grades and descriptions are used today as were used even before the publication of the first edition. Two things, however, have been added to the existing descriptions for describing the wear on coins. One addition has been the introduction of a numerical system for describing the amount of detail remaining on any coin. The numerical grading scale (1–70) was developed by Dr. W. Sheldon for grading and relating the prices of early US copper cents. Using his system, circulated coins are graded fron 1 to 59 and uncirculated coins are graded from 60 to 70. In general, the higher the number, the better the grade of the coin. Although the numerical scale is continuous, not all of its numbers are used—grading is simply not that precise. The grade of a Canadian coin is usually described by dealers, auction houses, etc. using the old adjectival term together with numerical scale equivalent, i.e. Extremely Fine-40, or EF-40.

The second major change to the grading scale has been the insertion of three "Choice" grades to the old adjectival scale to make the difference in wear between the higher grades more equal. This has eliminated the terms VF-EF, etc. from appearing in sales, etc. by adding a few new rungs to the grading ladder.

GRADING UNCIRCULATED COINS

An uncirculated coin must show no signs of wear or loss of detail because of wear when examined by the naked eye. An uncirculated coins is graded by assessing its lustre, the clarity of its surfaces and the fullness of its strike in relation to the typical mint state characteristics seen on a coin of that particular type.

Lustre

A coin with lustre that is dazzling and "alive" would have preference over one that is dull and lifeless. Mint lustre, or mint bloom, is a minute wrinkling of the surface of a new coin and is produced as the metal fills the die during the striking. It is beautiful to behold, especially on coins struck using high relief dies. Mint lustre is more delicate than the finest woodwork. Although relatively resistant to tarnish, the lustre is rapidly destroyed by any physical wear or harsh chemical action. Once removed, the bloom cannot be restored by any known method.

Surface

A coin with surfaces that are free of marks, or nearly so, is preferable to one with heavy bag and handling marks which detract from the overall beauty of the coin. Uncirculated coins are prone to receiving numerous dents, nicks and scratches before leaving the mint from falling into containers along with other coins, passing through coin counters, and being transported in bags. Before coins reach any bank they are often recounted and mechanically rolled for easier storage and handling. The blemishes so produced appear as bright spots or streaks against the softer sheen of the mint lustre. They are referred to as bag abrasions or bag marks and are easily distinguished from wear.

Strike

A well struck coin will exhibit all of the detail intended by the coin's engraver and is preferable to a coin which was poorly or weakly struck, with a resultant loss of detail in some areas. Convex surfaces on coins are often weak.

Each of the above factors is equally important in determining the grade of an uncirculated coin. In some cases, one factor may be so superior as to make up for a slight deficiency in one of the remaining two factors which, by itself, would lower the grade. When designating the grade for an uncirculated coin it is a common practice to prefix the letters MS (for Mint State) followed by the numerical grade. There are presently five recognized grades used to describe uncirculated coins. A brief description of each, along with its numerical grade, follows.

Typical Uncirculated (MS-60)

This grade refers to the typically seen uncirculated coin of the type and is expected to have a moderate but not excessive number of bag marks and rim nicks, although none of a serious nature. The lustre on the coin may be somewhat impaired by spotting or dullness. The strike may be weak enough for the coin to have a generalized weakness in detail in several areas. Usually, the impairments to any of these three factors will be obvious at first glance and will continue to distract from the overall appeal of the coin.

Select Uncirculated (MS-63)

A better example than a typical uncirculated coin but still lacking the appeal of a full Choice Uncirculated MS-65. The faults in the surface, lustre and strike are readily visible to the naked eye but, even collectively, they are not a major distraction to the overall appearance of the coin.

Choice Uncirculated (MS-65)

This grade is reserved for coins having an unquestionably quality appearance. Each of the three factors will be well above those exhibited by a typical mint state coin of the series. The strike is almost full except for slight weakness in a very localized area. The lustre will be almost completely free from impairments and the coin's surfaces will be generally free from marks except on the largest coins and those made of softer metal such as gold. Any slight imperfections in no way distract from the overall beauty of the coin.

Gem Uncirculated (MS-67)

This grade represents a coin which is essentially perfect in all respects to the naked eye. Only after extensive study is there likely to be any fault or criticism of the coin.

Perfect Uncirculated (MS-70)

This grade represents the finest quality available. A coin of this grade, examined under 4X magnification, will show no lines, marks or other evidence of handling or contact with other coins. The lustre will be of the highest quality possible, with no impairment of any sort. The strike will be full and sharp and of a quality higher than that usually found on coins of the series. The coin will display all of the detail intended by the engraver. The coin may be brilliant or lightly toned. However, if of copper or bronze, the coin must have full original lustre and colour (Full Red).

GRADING CIRCULATED COINS

Once a coin enters circulation, it begins to show physical wear on its surfaces. As time goes on, the coin becomes more and more worn until, after many decades, only the deepest of its original details remain. The extent of this wear is the primary factor determining the grade of circulated coins. There are ten grades currently used for describing circulated coins. A brief description of each, along with its numerical grade, follows.

About Good-3 (AG-3)

These very heavily worn coins are not listed in standard catalogues and only rareties are accepted in this grade by some collectors—usually as a filler until the same coin can be obtained in a higher grade. Portions of the design and legends are worn smooth and the date is barely discernible. Minor varieties are usually indistinguishable.

Good-4 (G-4)

This is the lowest grade usually listed in standard catalogues. The term "Good" is really a misnomer and "Poor" might be more apropos. Conservative collectors only accept rareties in this condition. The coin is heavily worn, with its major design visible but faint in some areas. Other features may be visible in outline form only with the central details worn away. Legends are considerably worn, but legible. Loss in weight begins to be significant.

Very Good-8 (VG-8)

The coin is considerably worn over its entire surface, with the higher portions of the designs worn through. The fine details in the hair, leaves, etc. are worn nearly smooth.

Fine-12 (F-12)

A coin in Fine condition shows moderate to considerable wear over its entire surfaces. The high areas of the designs are not worn through except for spots of high relief in exposed positions. Other details are clearer than on a Very Good example yet still not sharp. The entire design appears bold and all lettering is visible but with some weaknesses.

Very Fine-20 (VF-20)

A Very Fine coin shows clear evidence of circulation with clarity of detail. The high spots are worn, but not enough to obscure the detail. Other details are generally sharp, with traces of mint lustre lingering in sheltered places such as between the letters of the inscriptions.

Choice Very Fine-30 (VF-30)

This coin shows light even wear over its entire surfaces, with design details on the highest points slightly worn. All major features and lettering are still sharp.

Extremely Fine-40 (EF-40)

There is slight wear on the highest parts, with all other details clear and sharp. Traces of mint lustre are often present in places not subject to early wear.

Choice Extremely Fine-45 (EF-45)

The coin exhibits light overall wear on the highest parts of the design. All design details are very sharp and mint lustre can be seen in sheltered areas between the letters of the legends and around the edges.

About Uncirculated-50 (AU-50)

Traces of wear can be seen on nearly all of the highest areas of the design. The coin should exhibit at least half of the original mint lustre.

Choice About Uncirculated-55 (AU-55)

Only a small localized trace of wear on the highst points is visible to the naked eye.

ACKNOWLEDGEMENTS

The illustrations in the first edition were by artist Arthur Mueller. Additional illustrations by Patrick Glassford.

LARGE CENTS

Victoria 1858, 1859

On the obverse, an effigy of the Queen, laureate, appears within a beaded circle. The hair is tied in a knot at the back, leaving a pendant lock of hair. The hair at the temple is braided, the braid passing around and below the ear to the knot of hair. VICTORIA DEI GRATIA REGINA. with CANADA below.

The reverse displays ONE CENT and the date in three lines, within a beaded circle, enclosed by a continuoous wreath of maple leaves. Rim beads.

Points of wear: The eyebrow, the braid of hair below and in front of the ear and the laurel leaves nearest the ear. On the reverse, the wreath wears first. The obverse, being generally convex, is more than usually susceptible to wear.

ABOUT GOOD-3

All but the deepest details are gone. Legends begin to wear through.

GOOD-4

The braid of hair around the ear is worn through and nearly all the laurel leaves have been worn away. The facial features are blurred. On the reverse, the wreath is worn almost through and the legend is considerably worn. Circle and rim beads are blurred.

VERY GOOD-8

The eyebrow has worn away and no details remain in the braid around the ear. The laurel leaves are worn, those nearest the ear have been worn away. On the reverse, there is very little detail remaining in the wreath. The legend begins to thicken from wear. Circle and rim beads are blurred.

FINE-12

The eyebrow is indistinct and the braid begins to lose clarity, the segments beginning to merge into one another. The laurel leaves are worn, especially near the ear. On the reverse, the wreath is considerably worn but not worn through. Circle and rim beads begin to merge into one another.

VERY FINE-20

The eyebrow is considerably worn. The braid is worn, but each segment must be clearly, though not sharply, defined. The laurel leaves are clear but no longer sharp. On the reverse, the leaves of the wreath are worn but clear. Circle and rim beads are clear.

EXTREMELY FINE-40

The eyebrow is worn and the braid is slightly worn but clear. The laurel leaves are clear and sharp. On the reverse, the leaves of the wreath are slightly worn. Circle and rim beads are clear and sharp.

ABOUT UNCIRCULATED-50

There is slight wear on the eyebrow and parts of the braid. On the reverse, there is slight wear on the leaves of the wreath.

Victoria 1876–1901

The obverse shows a diademed effigy of the Queen to the left, within a beaded circle. The Queen's hair is tied in a knot at the back and bound with an ornamental hair band. The hair at the temple is brushed back over the ear and diadem to the knot at the back. Only the ear lobe is visible. Two ribbons hang down from the back, one turning outward and the other inward, overlapping the neck. VICTORIA DEI GRATIA REGINA. with CANADA below.

The reverse is the same as used on the cents of 1858 and 1859. Rim beads.

Points of wear: The eyebrow, the hair over the ear, the knot at the back (especially the bottom half), the jewels of the diadem, the details of the hair band and the end of the ribbon touching the neck. On the reverse, the leaves of the wreath and on convex reverses the word CENT (1892–1901).

ABOUT GOOD-3

Only the deepest details are visible. Legends are worn. On the reverse, the legend is often barely legible.

GOOD-4

The hair over the ear is worn through and there are no details in the knot at the back except the division between the two halves. Only part of the band of the diadem shows any details. Facial features are blurred and the legend is worn. On the reverse, virtually no details remain in the maple leaves and the legend is badly worn and often worn through on convex reverses. Circle and rim beads are blurred.

VERY GOOD-8

The eyebrow and ribbon end have been worn away and little or no detail remains in the hair over the ear or the bottom half of the knot at the back. The diadem is considerably worn, with some jewels partly worn off. The hair band is worn. On the reverse, there is little detail to the leaves of the wreath, while the legend is thickened and coarsened by wear. Circle and rim beads are blurred.

FINE-12

The eyebrow is almost worn through. Hair over the ear is worn, the strands beginning to run together. The bottom half of the knot is worn but the hair band is clear. The band of the diadem is clear but the jewels are worn. The ribbon end is indistinct. The legend is considerably worn on convex reverses, otherwise the wear is in the leaves of the wreath. Circle and rim beads begin to run together.

VERY FINE-20

The eyebrow is considerably worn, while the knot of hair at the back is clear but not sharp. The hair over the ear is clear. The jewels of the diadem are clear but not sharp. The ribbon end is worn but the hair band is clear and sharp. On the reverse, the leaves of the wreath are clear but not sharp, with a bit of wear on the outer edges. On convex reverses, light wear extends over the entire word CENT. Circle and rim beads are clear.

EXTREMELY FINE-40

The eyebrow is worn but the ribbon end is clear. The knot of hair, hair band, hair over the ear and the jewels of the diadem are all clear and sharp. On the reverse, there is very slight wear in the wreath and on convex reverses, slight wear on the N of CENT. Circle and rim beads are clear and sharp.

ABOUT UNCIRCULATED-50

There is very slight wear on the eyebrow and on the leaves of the wreath on the reverse.

Edward VII 1902–1910

The obverse features a crowned, robed effigy of the King to the right, within a beaded circle. The robe is fastened with the chain of the Order of the Garter, from a large bow on the shoulder. • EDWARDVS VII DEI GRATIA REX IMPERATOR • with CANADA below.

The reverse is the same as used on Victorian cents, with ONE CENT and the date in three lines within a beaded circle, enclosed by a continuous wreath of maple leaves. The reverses are convex until 1907. Rim beads.

Points of wear: The eyebrow, band of the crown, shoulder bow, ear and beard. On the reverse the leaves of the wreath and on convex reverses the word CENT.

ABOUT GOOD-3

All but the deepest details are gone. The legends begin to wear through. On the reverse the legend is barely legible.

GOOD-4

The band of the crown and the bow on the shoulder are worn through. The outer rim of the ear is worn off and little or no detail remains in the hair, beard, robe and chain. On the reverse, the legend is considerably worn, the word CENT being worn through on convex reverses. Little or no detail remains on the wreath. Circle and rim beads are badly blurred.

VERY GOOD-8

The eyebrow has been worn away. The band of the crown and the bow are worn through at their highest points. The outline of the ear is indistinct and the hair and beard are blurred. There is little detail to the robe and chain. On the reverse, there is little detail to the leaves of the wreath and the legend has been thickened and coarsened by wear, with the N of CENT worn through on convex reverses. Circle and rim beads are blurred.

FINE-12

There is considerable wear over the entire effigy, especially at the bow and the band of the crown. The jewels of the band will be slightly blurred. The legend is considerably worn on convex reverses. Otherwise the wear on the reverse occurs on the leaves of the wreath. Circle and rim beads begin to run together.

VERY FINE-20

The eyebrow is considerably worn and the bow shows wear. The hair, beard, band of crown and jewels are all clear but not sharp. On the reverse, the leaves are clear but not sharp, with a bit of wear on the outer edges. Convex reverses show wear over the word CENT. Circle and rim beads are clear but not sharp.

EXTREMELY FINE-40

The eyebrow is worn and there is slight wear on the bow and the band of the crown. The hair, beard, ear and the details of the robe and chain are all clear and sharp. On the reverse, there is very slight wear on the maple leaves and on convex reverses there is slight wear on the N of CENT. Circle and rim beads are clear and sharp.

ABOUT UNCIRCULATED-50

There is very slight wear on the eyebrow. Slight wear on the N of CENT may be seen on convex reverses.

George V 1911–1920

The obverse shows a robed, crowned effigy of the King to the left, wearing the chain of the Order of the Garter fastened by a bow on the shoulder. GEORGIVS V REX ET IND : IMP : in 1911; GEORGIVS V DEI GRA : REX ET IND : IMP : from 1912 to 1920.

The reverse shows ONE CENT CANADA and the date in four lines within a beaded circle, surrounded by a continuous wreath of maple leaves. Rim beads.

Points of wear: The eyebrow and the band of the crown; the wreath on the reverse. All dates are flat.

GOOD-4

There is little detail in the crown and very little detail in the robe. On the reverse, there is very little detail to the wreath and the legend is considerably worn.

VERY GOOD-8

The eyebrow has been worn away and the band of the crown is worn through in the middle. There is little detail to the hair, beard, chain and robe. On the reverse, the wreath shows considerable wear over its entire surface. The legend is coarsened. Circle and rim beads are blurred.

FINE-12

The eyebrow is indistinct. The band of the crown and its jewels are considerably worn, but only at the highest point. The band is not always worn through. The details of the chain and robe begin to blur. On the reverse, the leaves are considerably worn, mainly along the outer edges. The legend begins to thicken. Circle and rim beads begin to run together.

VERY FINE-20

The eyebrow is considerably worn. The band of the crown, jewels, hair, beard and the details of the chain and robe are clear but not sharp. The bow shows wear. On the reverse, the inscriptions are clear and the leaves show wear along the outer edges. Circle and rim beads are clear but not sharp.

EXTREMELY FINE-40

The eyebrow is worn. There is slight wear on the bow and the band of the crown. Other details are clear and sharp. On the reverse, the leaves of the wreath show the slightest wear and the legend is clear and sharp. Circle and rim beads are clear and sharp.

ABOUT UNCIRCULATED-50

There is slight wear on the eyebrow. On the reverse, slight wear may be seen on the wreath.

SMALL CENTS

George V 1920–1936

The obverse is the same as was described for the large cent, with the inscription GEORGIVS V DEI GRA: REX ET IND: IMP : .

The reverse shows ONE CENT in two lines, flanked by maple leaves. CANADA is curved to the top edge of the coin and the horizontal date appears at the bottom. There are no rim beads.

Points of wear: The points of wear on the obverse are similar to those on the large cent: the eyebrow, band of the crown and the details of the robe. On the reverse, the first places to wear are the edges of the maple leaves remote from the rim of the coin.

GOOD-4

Little detail remains in the crown and very little in the robe. On the reverse, the maple leaves show almost no detail and the legend is considerably worn.

VERY GOOD-8

The eyebrow has been worn away and the band of the crown is worn through in the middle. Little detail remains in the hair, beard, chain and robe. On the reverse, the legend is thickened by wear and the maple leaves retain little detail.

FINE-12

The eyebrow is indistinct. The band of the crown and jewels are considerably worn, but only at the highest point. The band is not always worn through. The details of the chain and robe begin to blur. The reverse shows wear over the entire design, but nothing has been worn away.

VERY FINE-20

The eyebrow is considerably worn and the bow shows wear. The band of the crown, jewels, robe, chain, hair and beard are all clear but not sharp. On the reverse, wear extends into the maple leaves from the edges remote from the rim and ONE CENT begins to show slight thickening.

EXTREMELY FINE-40

The eyebrow shows wear and there is also slight wear on the bow and the band of the crown. Other details are clear and sharp. On the reverse, only slight wear extends along the edges of the leaves remote from the rim.

ABOUT UNCIRCULATED-50

There is slight wear on the eyebrow. On the reverse, there is very slight wear on some portions of the edges of the maple leaves remote from the rim.

George VI 1937–1952

The obverse features a bare-headed effigy of the King to the left. GEORGIVS VI D : G : REX ET IND : IMP: from 1937 to 1947 and GEORGIVS VI DEI GRATIA REX from 1948 to 1952.

The reverse depicts two large maple leaves on a common twig, with 1CENT above and the date below. CANADA is curved to the bottom edge of the coin. Beaded rims.

Points of wear: The eyebrow and ear lobe, the hair above the ear, and the hairline at the temple and at the back of the neck. On the reverse, the bottom of the leaves show wear first.

VERY GOOD-8

There are no details in the hair above the ear and very little detail remains on the ear. On the reverse, the legend is thickened by wear and the maple leaves retain little detail.

FINE-12

The eyebrow has been worn away. There is little detail in the hair above the ear. The hairlines at the temple and at the back of the neck are indistinct. The ear is considerably worn. On the reverse, the ridges separating the segments of the leaves have been considerably widened by wear. The rim beads begin to run together.

VERY FINE-20

The eyebrow is indistinct and the hair above the ear is considerably worn. The hairlines at the temple and at the back of the neck are rather blurred. Elsewhere the hair is clear but not sharp. The outer rim of the ear shows wear extending up from the lobe. On the reverse, the ridges separating the segments of the leaves are worn and the veins are clear but not sharp. Wear extends from the bottom into the centre of the leaves. The rim beads are clear.

EXTREMELY FINE-40

There is wear on the eyebrow and slight wear on the hair at the temple and above the ear, with a spot of wear on the ear lobe. Other details are clear and sharp. On the reverse, the maple leaves show slight wear along their bottom edges. Other details are clear and sharp.

ABOUT UNCIRCULATED-50

There is slight wear on the eyebrow and on the ear lobe. On the reverse, there are traces of wear on the bottom edges of the maple leaves.

Elizabeth II 1953–1964

The obverse features a draped, laureate effigy of the Queen to the right. ELIZABETH II DEI GRATIA REGINA.

The reverse is the same as the George VI cents, showing two large maple leaves on a common twig, with 1CENT above and the date below. CANADA is curved to the bottom edge of the coin. Beaded rims.

Points of wear: The middle leaves of the laurel wreath, the eyebrow, the hair around the ear and the lines of drapery over the shoulder. The reverse shows wear first on the bottom edges of the leaves.

FINE-12

The eyebrow is indistinct and the laurel wreath is worn almost through. The lines in the drapery are indistinct. On the reverse, the ridges separating the segments of the leaves have been considerably widened by wear. The rim beads begin to run together.

VERY FINE-20

The eyebrow is considerably worn. The laurel wreath is worn and the hair above the ear shows wear extending toward the forehead. The lines of the drapery are clear. On the reverse, the ridges separating the segments of the leaves are worn, while the veins are clear but not sharp. Wear extends from the bottom into the centre of the leaves. The rim beads are clear.

EXTREMELY FINE-40

The eyebrow is worn. There is slight wear on the laurel leaves and the hair above the ear. The lines of the drapery are clear and sharp. On the reverse, the maple leaves are slightly worn along their bottom edges. The other details remain clear and sharp.

ABOUT UNCIRCULATED-50

There is slight wear on the eyebrow. On the reverse, there are traces of wear on the bottom edges of the maple leaves.

Elizabeth II 1965–1989
(Excluding 1967 commemorative issue)

The obverse displays a more mature effigy of the Queen to the right, draped and wearing a diamond tiara. ELIZABETH II is curved to the left edge and D • G • REGINA is curved to the right. The device was slightly reduced in size in 1979.

The reverse again features the familiar maple twig design.

In 1982 the obverse and reverse rim beads were replaced with beaded borders, moved inward from the rim and the shape of the coin was changed to twelve-sided.

Points of wear: The eyebrow, the hair concealing the top of the ear, the hair at the temple and forehead and the centre of the band of the tiara; also the drapery over the shoulder, particularly the line marking the top of the Queen's gown. On the reverse, the bottom edges of the maple leaves will wear first.

EXTREMELY FINE-40

There is slight wear on the eyebrow, the hair covering the ear, the centre of the tiara and the hair at the temple, forehead and cheek. The drapery over the shoulder will show slight wear, particularly the line marking the top of the Queen's gown. On the reverse, there is slight wear on the bottom edges of the maple leaves.

ABOUT UNCIRCULATED-50

There is a trace of wear on the eyebrow. On the reverse, there are traces of wear on the bottom edges of the maple leaves.

Elizabeth II 1967

The obverse is the same as described for 1965–1989. To commemorate the centennial of Confederation a different animal motif was used on the reverse of each denomination. The reverse of the one cent features a rock dove in flight, with 1 CENT curved to the top and CANADA 1867-1967 curved to the bottom edge of the coin.

Points of wear: The reverse shows wear first on the small feathers on the breast of the dove, then on the head. Wear then begins at the wing tips and spreads towards the body, The tail feathers are the last to show wear.

Elizabeth II 1990–

The obverse features a contemporary effigy of the Queen, wearing a necklace, earring and an elaborate crown. ELIZABETH II is curved to the left edge and D • G • REGINA is curved to the right. The figure is truncated at the base of the neck. The reverse design is the same as previous Elizabethan cents.

In 1997 the shape of the cent was changed from 12-sided to round.

Points of wear: The hair covering the band of the crown near the ear; the hair between the front of the crown and the forehead; and the back of the queen's shoulder where the truncation begins. On the reverse, the bottom of the maple leaves will wear first.

SILVER FIVE CENTS

Victoria 1858–1901

The obverse displays an effigy of the Queen to the left, laureate, with the hair tied in a knot or chignon at the back, leaving a pendant lock of hair. The hair at the temple is braided, the braid passing around and below the ear to the knot of hair. VICTORIA DEI GRATIA REGINA. with CANADA below.

The reverse displays 5 CENTS and the date in three lines, within a wreath of maple leaves, surmounted by St. Edward's crown. Beaded rims.

Points of wear: The eyebrow, the braid of hair below and in front of the ear; the knot of hair at the back and the laurel leaves nearest the ear. On the reverse, wear begins on the crown and the wreath leaves immediately flanking the bow. Convex reverses will wear first at the N of CENTS.

ABOUT GOOD-3

All but the deepest details are gone. On the reverse, the legend is barely legible.

GOOD-4

The braid of the hair and the laurel leaves nearest the ear are worn through. The knot of hair at the back is badly worn and the facial features are blurred. On the reverse, there are no details to the wreath or crown and the legend is sometimes worn through. Rim beads are indistinct.

VERY GOOD-8

The eyebrow has been worn away and no detail remains in the braid around the ear. The laurel leaves are considerably worn, those nearest the ear being almost worn through. There is little detail to the knot of hair. On the reverse, there is little detail remaining in the wreath or crown. The legend is badly worn on convex reverses.

29

FINE-12

The eyebrow is indistinct and the segments of the braid begin to run together, those nearest the ear being considerably worn. The laurel leaves are somewhat worn, especially near the ear and the segments of the knot begin to merge. On the reverse, all the leaves are worn; the outer third of the top leaves and the outer half of the bottom leaves. The pearls in the arches of the crown begin to merge into one another. The legend shows general wear, the N of CENTS being considerably worn on convex reverses. Rim beads begin to merge.

VERY FINE-20

The eyebrow is considerably worn. The segments ot the braid are clear but not sharp, those nearest the ear sometimes beginning to run together. The laurel leaves are clear but not sharp; those above the ear are sometimes a bit blurred. On the reverse, wear extends up the sides of the wreath, the outer third or so of the bottom leaves being considerably worn. The other details are clear.

EXTREMELY FINE-40

The eyebrow is worn. The braid is slightly worn but generally clear and sharp. The laurel leaves are clear and sharp, only those next to the ear showing any wear. On the reverse, there is slight wear on the outer edges of the leaves, especially the bottom leaves. Other details are clear and sharp.

ABOUT UNCIRCULATED-50

There is slight wear on the eyebrow and very slight wear on the laurel leaves above the ear. On the reverse, there is slight wear on the bottom leaves of the wreath.

Edward VII 1902–1910

The obverse bears a crowned, robed effigy of the King to the right, wearing the chain of the Order of the Garter fastened by a bow on the shoulder. EDWARDVS VII D.G. REX IMPERATOR.

The reverse displays 5 CENTS CANADA and the date, in four lines within a wreath of maple leaves and surmounted by a stylized Imperial State Crown. Beaded rims.

Points of wear: The eyebrow, band of the crown, bow on the shoulder, ear and beard. On the reverse, the crown and the bottom leaves of the wreath are the first to wear. Reverses are generally concave until 1906, after which year the coins are flat.

ABOUT GOOD-3

All but the deepest details are gone from both sides. The reverse legend is barely legible.

GOOD-4

The band of the crown, the bow on the shoulder and the outer rim of the ear are worn through. There is little detail remaining in the robe, chain, hair and beard. On the reverse, the crown is badly worn and the leaves of the wreath show little detail. Rim beads are blurred.

VERY GOOD-8

The eyebrow has been worn away and the band of the crown is worn through in the middle. The bow is partly worn through and little detail remains on the chain and robe. The hair and beard are considerably worn and the outline of the ear is indistinct. On the reverse, the pearls in the arches of the crown are blurred and the central arch is often worn through. Little detail remains in the leaves of the wreath. Rim beads are blurred.

FINE-12

The eyebrow is indistinct; the band of the crown and its jewels are considerably worn as is the bow on the shoulder. On convex obverses the band of the crown is sometimes worn through. On the reverse, the pearls in the arches of the crown begin to merge and the central arch is considerably worn. The bottom leaves of the wreath are worn to the extent of half of their area and the other leaves to about a third. Rim beads begin to merge.

VERY FINE-20

The eyebrow is considerably worn. The band of the crown and its jewels are clear but not sharp. The hair, beard and bow are slightly worn, while the details of the robe and chain are clear but not sharp. On the reverse, the outer third or so of the bottom leaves is worn and the central arch of the crown shows wear along its entire length. Rim beads are clear.

EXTREMELY FINE-40

The eyebrow is worn and slight wear can be seen on the crown and shoulder bow. Other details remain clear and sharp. On the reverse, the bottom leaves are only slightly worn and the central arch of the crown shows a spot of wear. Rim beads are clear and sharp.

ABOUT UNCIRCULATED-50

There is slight wear on the eyebrow and on the highest point in the band of the crown. On the reverse, the bottom leaves show slight wear on the edges nearest the rim.

George V 1911–1921

The obverse shows an effigy of the King to the left, robed and crowned, wearing the chain of the Order of the Garter fastened by a bow on the shoulder. GEORGIVS V REX ET IND:IMP: in 1911 and GEORGIVS V DEI GRA: REX ET IND:IMP: from 1912 to 1921.

The reverse shows 5 CENTS CANADA and the date, in four lines, within a wreath of maple leaves and surmounted by a stylized Imperial State Crown. Beaded rims.

Points of wear: The eyebrow, band of the crown and bow on the shoulder. On the reverse, the leaves of the wreath, especially at the bottom, are vulnerable. The word CENTS is subject to early wear on convex reverses.

ABOUT GOOD-3

All but the deepest details are gone from both sides. The reverse legend is barely legible.

GOOD-4

The band of the crown and the bow are worn through and there is little detail to the robe. On the reverse, very little detail remains in the wreath. The legend is badly worn on convex reverses. Rim beads are blurred.

VERY GOOD-8

The eyebrow has been worn away. The band of the crown and the jewels are considerably worn, being worn through at the middle. Little detail remains in the robe and the bow is considerably worn. On the reverse, the pearls in the arches of the crown are blurred, and the central arch is often worn through. Little detail remains in the leaves of the wreath and the N of CENTS may be worn through on convex reverses. Rim beads are blurred.

FINE-12

The eyebrow is indistinct while the band of the crown and the jewels are worn. The details of the robe and chain begin to blur. The bow is worn and the rim beads begin to merge. On the reverse, the bottom leaves of the wreath are worn to about half their area and the others to about a third. The central arch of the crown is considerably worn and the pearls in the arches begin to run together. Rim beads begin to run together.

VERY FINE-20

The eyebrow is considerably worn. The band of the crown, its jewels and the bow are all clear but not sharp. On the reverse, the outer third or so of the bottom leaves are worn and the central arch of the crown is slightly worn along its entire length. Rim beads are clear.

EXTREMELY FINE-40

The eyebrow is worn and there is slight wear along the band of the crown. Other details are clear and sharp. On the reverse, the bottom leaves of the wreath are slightly worn and the central arch of the crown shows a spot of wear. Rim beads are clear and sharp.

ABOUT UNCIRCULATED-50

There is slight wear on the eyebrow and very slight wear on the centre of the band of the crown. On the reverse, there is very slight wear on the central arch of the crown.

NICKEL, TOMBAC AND STEEL FIVE CENTS

George V 1922–1936

All the five-cent pieces of George V were struck in nickel and are round in shape. The obverse depicts the familiar robed, crowned effigy of the King to the left. GEORGIVS V DEI GRA: REX ET IND: IMP: .

The reverse shows FIVE5CENTS, with CANADA curved to the top edge of the coin and the date curved to the bottom edge beneath two large maple leaves. There are no rim beads on either side.

Points of wear: The eyebrow, band of the crown, bow, robe and chain. On the reverse, the edges, on the maple leaves, nearest the large numeral 5 are the first to wear.

GOOD-4

Little detail remains on the crown and robe. On the reverse, the maple leaves show very little detail, the edges beginning to wear through. The large numeral 5 is considerably coarsened by wear.

VERY GOOD-8

The eyebrow has been worn away. The band of the crown is worn through in the middle and only a little detail remains in the robe. The chain, hair and beard are badly worn. On the reverse, the maple leaves are considerably worn, but the edges are not worn through. The large numeral 5 is thickened by wear.

FINE-12

The eyebrow is indistinct. The band of the crown and the jewels are considerably worn and the details of the robe and chain begin to blur. On the reverse, there is wear over the entire surface, but details are clear except on the edges of the maple leaves nearest the large 5.

VERY FINE-20

The eyebrow is considerably worn and the bow shows wear. The band of the crown, jewels, robe, chain, hair and beard are clear but not sharp. On the reverse, wear extends into the centre of the maple leaves and the large numeral 5 shows slight wear.

EXTREMELY FINE-40

The eyebrow shows wear and there is slight wear on the bow and the band of the crown. Other details are clear and sharp. On the reverse, there is slight wear along the edges of the maple leaves nearest the large numeral 5.

ABOUT UNCIRCULATED-50

There is slight wear on the eyebrow. On the reverse, there is very slight wear on the edges of the maple leaves nearest the large numeral 5.

George VI 1937–1952
(Excluding 1943–1945)

The five-cent piece was round until late in 1942 when the shape was changed to twelve-sided. It remained twelve-sided for the balance of the reign.

The coins were struck in nickel from 1937 to 1942 and from 1946 to 1950; all issues wearing the same as described here. An alloy of copper and tin, called tombac, was used for the 12-sided issue of 1942. The designs were the same as previous except for the shape of the coins and the lack of rim beads. In 1951 and 1952 the beaver five cent pieces were coined in chrome-plated steel. These wear the same as the nickel coinages but more slowly because of the harder surfaces. One point of caution is necessary. When looking for uncirculated specimens, a collector must always look at the edge of the coin where any wear will appear as spots where the chrome plating has worn away. An uncirculated specimen must not show any spots along the edge or rim where the plating has worn off.

The obverse shows a bare-headed effigy of the King, to the left. GEORGIVS VI D:G:REX ET IND:IMP:from 1937 to 1947 and GEORGIVS VI DEI GRATIA REX from 1948 to 1952.

The reverse shows a beaver on a rock, with its forepaws on a log to the left. 5 CENTS, flanked by two small maple leaves is curved to the top edge while CANADA and the date appear in two lines in the exergue. Beaded rims.

Points of wear: The eyebrow and ear lobe, the hair above the ear and the hairline at the temple and at the back of the neck. On the reverse, the beaver's haunch, abdomen and upper foreleg wear first.

VERY GOOD-8

There is little detail in the hair or the rim of the ear and the facial features begin to coarsen. On the reverse, the body of the beaver shows little detail, while the details of the tail, log and rock are indistinct. Rim beads are blurred.

FINE-12

The eyebrow has been worn away and little detail remains in the hair above the ear. The hairline is indistinct at the temple and at the back of the neck. The ear is considerably worn. On the reverse, the haunch, abdomen and foreleg are considerably worn. The rock, log and the hair on the beaver's back begin to blur. Rim beads begin to blur.

VERY FINE-20

The eyebrow is indistinct and the hair above the ear is considerably worn. The hairline is rather blurred at the temple and the back of the neck. The outer rim of the ear shows wear up from the lobe. On the reverse, the beaver's abdomen and foreleg show wear and the haunch is definitely worn. Other details are clear but not sharp. Rim beads are clear.

EXTREMELY FINE-40

There is wear on the eyebrow. Slight wear can be seen on the hair at the temple and over the ear, with a spot of wear on the ear lobe. Other details are clear and sharp. On the reverse, there is slight wear at the beaver's haunch.

ABOUT UNCIRCULATED-50

There is slight wear on the ear lobe. On the reverse, there is very slight wear on the haunch of the beaver.

George VI 1943–1945

The 1943–1945 issues display a 'Victory' reverse instead of the familiar beaver. The 1943 issue was once again struck in tombac. Because the alloy was unpopular, the 1944 and 1945 coins were struck in chrome-plated steel. Again, uncirculated specimens must not show spots where the chrome plating has been worn away.

The obverse bears the familiar bare-headed effigy of the the King to the left. GEORGIVS VI D : G : REX ET IND : IMP :. Rim beads on the obverse.

The reverse shows a lighted torch superimposed on a large V with two digits of the date to either side. CANADA is curved above and CENTS flanked by maple leaves, is curved below. Instead of rim beads, WE WIN WHEN WE WORK WILLINGLY appears in Morse Code as a border against the rim. The coins are twelve-sided.

Points of wear: The eyebrow and ear lobe; the hair at the temple, above the ear and at the back of the neck. On the reverse, the shaft of the torch and the arms of the V are the first to wear.

VERY GOOD-8

There is little detail to the hair and the rim of the ear and the facial features begin to coarsen. On the reverse, the shaft of the torch shows little detail and the arms of the V are considerably worn. The coded border is worn.

FINE-12

The eyebrow has been worn away and there is little detail in the hair above the ear. The hairlines at the temple and the back of the neck are indistinct. The ear is considerably worn. On the reverse, the torch is considerably worn and the arms of the V are worn right to the angle. The coded border is slightly blurred.

VERY FINE-20

The eyebrow is indistinct and the hair above the ear is considerably worn. The hairline is rather blurred at the temple and the back of the neck. The outer rim of the ear shows wear up from the lobe. On the reverse, the torch is worn but clear. The arms of the V show slight wear. The coded border is still clear and sharp.

EXTREMELY FINE-40

There is wear on the eyebrow. There is slight wear in the hair at the temple and above the ear, with a spot of wear on the ear lobe. On the reverse, the torch is slightly worn and other details are clear and sharp. The coded border is clear and sharp. The chrome plating may be worn through at the angles of the rim.

ABOUT UNCIRCULATED-50

There is slight wear on the ear lobe. On the reverse, there is very slight wear at the angles of the rim.

George VI 1951

The obverse bears the familiar effigy of the King to the left. GEORGIVS VI DEI GRATIA REX.

The reverse features the simplified outline of a nickel smelter. CANADA is curved at the top, with the smoke stack from the smelter passing between the letters N and A. NICKEL 1751–1951 lies to the left of the stack in two lines and 5 CENTS appears in two lines to the right of the stack. Three maple leaves are shown in the exergue. Beaded rims. The coin is twelve-sided.

Points of wear: The eyebrow and ear lobe; the hair at the temple, above the ear and at the back of the neck. On the reverse, the smelter's roof and stack and the outer edges of the maple leaves are the first to wear.

FINE-12

The eyebrow has worn away and little detail remains in the hair above the ear. The hairline is indistinct at the temple and at the back of the neck. The ear is considerably worn. On the reverse, the stack is considerably thickened by wear and the maple leaves are worn inward from their outer edges to about a quarter of their area.

VERY FINE-20

The eyebrow is indistinct and the hair above the ear is considerably worn. The hairline is rather blurred at the temple and the back of the neck. The outer rim of the ear shows wear extending up from the lobe. On the reverse, the stack and roof are clearly but not sharply outlined. The edges of the leaves are a little worn.

EXTREMELY FINE-40

The eyebrow is worn. There is slight wear in the hair at the temple and above the ear, with a spot of wear on the ear lobe. On the reverse, there is slight wear at the bottom of the stack and the centre of the roof, while the maple leaves show faint signs of wear.

ABOUT UNCIRCULATED-50

There is slight wear on the eyebrow and ear lobe. On the reverse, there is very slight wear on the outer edges of the maple leaves.

STEEL, NICKEL AND CUPRO-NICKEL FIVE CENTS

Elizabethan five-cent pieces were struck in steel until 1964 and in nickel from 1965 to 1981. Five-cent pieces have been composed of cupro-nickel since 1982. The coins were 12-sided until 1962 but have been round in shape since 1963.

Elizabeth II 1953–1964

The obverse shows a draped, laureate effigy of the Queen to the right. ELIZABETH II DEI GRATIA REGINA. The reverse again shows the familiar beaver design with 5 CENTS. flanked by maple leaves, curved to the top edge and with CANADA and the date, in two lines, in the exergue. The coins are round with rim beads on both sides.

Points of wear: The middle leaves of the laurel wreath, the hair about the ear, the eyebrow and the lines of the drapery on the shoulder. On the reverse, the beaver's haunch, abdomen and upper foreleg are the first to show wear.

FINE-12

The eyebrow has been worn away and the laurel leaves are worn almost through. The lines of the drapery are indistinct. On the reverse, the beaver's haunch, abdomen and foreleg are considerably worn. The hair on the beaver's back begins to blur. The rock and log begin to blur. Rim beads begin to merge.

VERY FINE-20

The eyebrow is considerably worn. The laurel leaves are worn and the wear on the hair above the ear extends toward the forehead. The lines of the drapery are clear. On the reverse, the beaver's haunch is definitely worn and the abdomen and foreleg show wear. Other details are clear. The rim beads are clear.

EXTREMELY FINE-40

The eyebrow is worn and there is slight wear on the hair and laurel leaves above the ear. The drapery is clear and sharp. On the reverse, there is slight wear at the beaver's haunch.

ABOUT UNCIRCULATED-50

There is slight wear on the eyebrow and the laurel leaves above the ear. On the reverse, there is very slight wear on the haunch of the beaver.

Elizabeth II 1965–1989
(Excluding 1967 commemorative issue)

The obverse shows a more mature, draped effigy of the Queen, to the right, wearing a diamond tiara. ELIZABETH II curved to the left edge and D • G • REGINA curved to the right.
 The reverse bears the familiar beaver design.

Points of wear: The eyebrow, the hair concealing the top of the ear, the hair at the temple and forehead and the centre of the band of the tiara. The drapery over the shoulder, particularly the line marking the top of the Queen's gown. On the reverse, the beaver's haunch, abdomen and upper foreleg will show the first wear.

EXTREMELY FINE-40

There is slight wear on the eyebrow, the hair concealing the top of the ear and the hair at the temple and forehead. There is slight wear on the centre of the tiara and on the cheek. The drapery over the shoulder shows slight wear, particularly the line marking the top of the Queen's gown. On the reverse there is slight wear at the beaver's haunch.

ABOUT UNCIRCULATED-50

There is a trace of wear on the eyebrow. On the reverse, there is very slight wear at the haunch of the beaver.

Elizabeth II 1967

The obverse is the same as described for 1965–1989. To commemorate the centennial of Confederation a different animal motif was used on the reverse of each denomination. The reverse of the five-cent piece features a hopping rabbit, with 5 CENTS curved to the top and CANADA 1867-1967 curved to the bottom edge of the coin.

Points of wear: On the reverse, the rabbit first shows wear on the front shoulder and at the highest point on the haunch, then spreads towards the head and the tail.

Elizabeth II 1990–

The obverse features a contemporary effigy of the Queen, to the right, wearing a necklace, an earring and an elaborate crown. ELIZABETH II is curved to the left edge and D • G • REGINA is curved to the right. The figure is truncated at the base of the neck. The reverse bears the familiar beaver design.

Points of wear: The hair covering the band of the crown near the ear; the hair between the front of the crown and the forehead; and the back of the queen's shoulder where the truncation begins. On the reverse, the beaver's haunch, abdomen and upper foreleg are the first to show wear.

SILVER TEN CENTS

Victoria 1858–1901

The obverse displays an effigy of the Queen to the left, laureate, with the hair tied in a knot or chignon at the back, leaving a pendant lock of hair. The hair at the temple is braided, the braid passing around and below the ear to the knot of hair. VICTORIA DEI GRATIA REGINA. with CANADA below.

The reverse displays 10 CENTS and date in three lines, within a wreath of maple leaves, surmounted by St. Edward's crown. Beaded rims.

Points of wear: The eyebrow, the braid of hair below and in front of the ear. On the reverse, wear begins on the crown and the wreath leaves immediately flanking the bow. Convex reverses will wear first at the N of CENTS.

ABOUT GOOD-3

All but the deepest details are gone. On the reverse, the legend is barely legible.

GOOD-4

The braid of the hair and the laurel leaves near the ear are worn through. The knot of hair at the back is badly worn. The facial features are blurred. On the reverse, there are no details to the wreath or crown and the legend is sometimes worn through, especially on convex reverses. Rim beads are indistinct.

VERY GOOD-8

The eyebrow has been worn away and no details remain in the braid around the ear. The laurel leaves are considerably worn, those nearest the ear being almost worn through. There is little detail to the knot of hair. On the reverse, there is little detail remaining in the wreath or crown. The legend is badly worn on convex reverses.

FINE-12

The eyebrow is indistinct and the segments of the braid begin to run together. The laurel leaves are somewhat worn, especially near the ear and segments of the knot begin to merge. On the reverse, all the leaves are worn, the outer third of the top leaves and the outer half of the bottom ones. The pearls in the arches of the crown and the rim beads begin to merge into one another. The legend shows general wear, the N of CENTS being considerably worn on convex reverses.

VERY FINE-20

The eyebrow is considerably worn. The segments of the braid are clear but not sharp, those above the ear are sometimes a bit blurred. On the reverse, wear extends up the leaves of the wreath, the outer third or so of the bottom leaves being considerably worn. The other details are clear.

EXTREMELY FINE-40

The eyebrow is worn. The braid is slightly worn but generally clear and sharp. The laurel leaves are clear and sharp, only those next to the ear showing any wear. On the reverse, there is slight wear on the edges of the leaves nearest the rim, especially the bottom leaves. Other details are clear and sharp.

ABOUT UNCIRCULATED-50

There is slight wear on the eyebrow and the laurel leaves nearest the ear. On the reverse, there is slight wear on the bottom leaves of the wreath.

Edward VII 1902–1910

The obverse effigy depicts the King to the right, robed, crowned and wearing the chain of the Order of the Garter fastened by a bow on the shoulder. EDWARDVS VII D.G. REX IMPERATOR

The reverse shows 10 CENTS CANADA and the date in four lines, within a wreath of maple leaves and surmounted by a stylized Imperial State crown. Beaded rims.

Points of wear: The eyebrow, the band of the crown, the bow on the shoulder, the ear and the beard. On the reverse, the crown and the bottom leaves of the wreath are the first places to wear. Reverses are generally concave until 1906, after which year the coins are flat.

ABOUT GOOD-3

All but the deepest details are gone. On the reverse, the legend is barely legible.

GOOD-4

The band of the crown, the bow on the shoulder and the outer rim of the ear are worn through. There is little detail to the robe, chain, hair and beard. On the reverse, the crown is badly worn and the leaves of the wreath show little detail. Rim beads are blurred.

VERY GOOD-8

The eyebrow has been worn away and the band of the crown is worn through in the middle. The bow is also worn through and little detail on the chain and robe remains. The hair and beard are considerably worn and the outline of the ear is indistinct. On the reverse, the pearls in the arches of the crown are blurred and the central arch is often worn through. There is little detail remaining in the leaves of the wreath. Rim beads are blurred.

FINE-12

The eyebrow is indistinct. The band of the crown, the jewels and the bow on the shoulder are considerably worn. On convex obverses, the band of the crown is sometimes worn through. The hair and beard are worn. On the reverse, the pearls in the arches of the crown begin to merge and the central arch is considerably worn. The bottom leaves of the wreath are worn to the extent of half their area and the other leaves to about a third. Rim beads begin to merge.

VERY FINE-20

The eyebrow is considerably worn. The band of the crown and the jewels are clear but not sharp. The hair and beard are slightly worn. The bow is worn and the details of the robe and chain are clear but not sharp. On the reverse, the outer third or so of the bottom leaves is worn and the central arch of the crown shows wear along its entire length. Rim beads are clear.

EXTREMELY FINE-40

The eyebrow is worn and there is slight wear on the band of the crown and the shoulder bow. The other details are clear and sharp. On the reverse, the bottom leaves are only slightly worn and the central arch of the crown shows a spot of wear. Rim beads are clear and sharp.

ABOUT UNCIRCULATED-50

There is slight wear on the eyebrow and on the band of the crown at its highest point. On the reverse, the bottom leaves show traces of wear on the edges nearest the rim.

George V 1911–1936

The obverse effigy depicts the King to the left, crowned and robed, the robe being fastened by the chain of the Order of the Garter by means of a bow on the shoulder. GEORGIVS V REX ET IND: IMP: in 1911 and GEORGIVS V DEI GRA: REX ET IND: IMP: from 1912 to 1936.

The reverse displays 10 CENTS CANADA and the date in four lines, within a wreath of maple leaves and surmounted by a stylized Imperial State Crown. Beaded rims.

Points of wear: The eyebrow, the band of the crown and the bow on the shoulder. On the reverse, the leaves of the wreath, especially those at the bottom, are vulnerable. The word CENTS is subject to early wear on convex reverses.

ABOUT GOOD-3

All but the deepest details are gone. On the reverse, the legend is barely legible.

GOOD-4

Both the band of the crown and the shoulder bow are worn through and there is little detail to the robe. On the reverse, there is very little detail to the leaves in the wreath and the legend is badly worn on convex reverses. Rim beads are blurred.

VERY GOOD-8

The eyebrow has been worn away. The band of the crown and the jewels are considerably worn through the middle. There is little detail to the robe and the bow is considerably worn. On the reverse, the pearls in the arches of the crown are blurred and the central arch is often worn through. There is little detail to the leaves in the wreath. The word CENTS may be worn through at the N on convex reverses. Rim beads are blurred.

FINE-12

The eyebrow is indistinct. The band of the crown and the jewels are worn. The details of the robe and chain begin to blur. The bow is worn. On the reverse, the bottom leaves of the wreath are worn to about half their area, the others to about a third. The central arch of the crown is considerably worn and the pearls in the arches begin to run together. Rim beads begin to merge.

VERY FINE-20

The eyebrow is considerably worn. The band of the crown, jewels and shoulder bow are all clear but not sharp. On the reverse, the outer third or so of the bottom leaves is worn while the central arch of the crown is slightly worn along its entire length. Rim beads are clear.

EXTREMELY FINE-40

The eyebrow is slightly worn and there is slight wear along the band of the crown. Other details are clear and sharp. On the reverse, the bottom leaves of the wreath are slightly worn and the central arch of the crown shows a spot of wear. Rim beads are clear and sharp.

ABOUT UNCIRCULATED-50

There is slight wear on the eyebrow and very slight wear on the band of the crown at its centre. On the reverse, there is slight wear on the central arch of the crown and on the edges of the bottom leaves nearest the rim.

George VI 1937–1952

The obverse shows the King, bare-headed and facing left. The effigy is truncated at the base of the neck. GEORGIVS VI D : G : REX ET IND : IMP : from 1937 to 1947, and GEORGIVS VI DEI GRATIA REX from 1948 to 1952.

The reverse depicts a fishing schooner saling to the left, with CANADA curved to the top edge while 10 CENTS appears horizontally in the exergue. The date is shown to the right of the schooner. In 1937, the date is in smaller numerals and closer to the water than other years.

Points of wear: The eyebrow and earlobe, the hair above the ear and the hairline at the temple and at the back of the neck. On the reverse, the jib, the stays and shrouds and the line separating the hull from the water.

VERY GOOD-8

There is little detail in the hair or the rim of the ear. The facial features begin to coarsen. On the reverse, the stays and shrouds are worn through and the sails begin to merge into one another. The legends are considerably worn. On pieces dated 1937, the date, although considerably thickened by wear, must be legible.

FINE-12

The eyebrow has been worn away and there is little detail in the hair above the ear. The hairline is indistinct at the temple and the back of the neck. The ear is considerably worn. On the reverse, the sails are worn and the rigging is indistinct. 10 CENTS is worn and the line separating the hull from the water is indistinct. On pieces dated 1937, the date must be clear for the piece to be considered fine. It may be somewhat thickened by wear, but must be legible.

VERY FINE-20

The eyebrow is indistinct and the hair above the ear is considerably worn. The hairline is rather blurred at the temple and the back of the neck. The outer rim of the ear shows wear up from the lobe. On the reverse, wear extends over most of the jib. The rigging and the line separating the hull from the water are clear but by no means sharp. 10 CENTS begins to show wear.

EXTREMELY FINE-40

The eyebrow is worn and there is slight wear in the hair at the temple and above the ear, with a spot of wear on the ear lobe. There is wear on the hair line at the temple and the back of the neck. Other details are clear and sharp. On the reverse, there is slight wear on the jib. The rigging and other details are clear and sharp.

ABOUT UNCIRCULATED-50

There is a trace of wear on the ear lobe. On the reverse, there are traces of wear over the jib.

Elizabeth II 1953–1964

The obverse effigy depicts the Queen to the right, draped and laureate. ELIZABETH II DEI GRATIA REGINA.

The reverse is the same schooner design as shown on the George VI issues. Beaded rims.

Points of wear: The middle leaves of the laurel wreath, the hair about the ear, the eyebrow and the lines of drapery on the shoulder. On the reverse, the jib, the stays and shrouds and the line separating the hull from the water.

FINE-12

The eyebrow has been worn away and the laurel wreath is worn almost through. The shoulder drapery is indistinct. On the reverse, the rigging and the line separating the hull from the water are indistinct. 10 CENTS is worn. Rim beads begin to merge.

VERY FINE-20

The eyebrow is considerably worn. The laurel wreath is worn and wear on the hair over the ear extends toward the forehead. The lines of the drapery are clear. On the reverse, wear extends over most of the lower sails. The rigging and the line separating the hull from the water are clear, but by no means sharp. 10 CENTS begins to wear. Rim beads are clear.

EXTREMELY FINE-40

The eyebrow is worn and there is slight wear on the hair and the laurel leaves above the ear. The drapery is clear and sharp. On the reverse, there is slight wear on the jib. The rigging and other details are clear and sharp. Rim beads are clear and sharp.

ABOUT UNCIRCULATED-50

There is slight wear on the eyebrow. On the reverse, there are traces of wear on the jib.

SILVER AND NICKEL TEN CENTS

The mint continued to strike the ten-cent pieces in .800 silver until mid-1967 when the composition was changed to .500 silver and approximately half of that year's production was struck in each alloy. Early 1968 production was begun in .500 silver, but the composition was changed to nickel during the year and has remained the same since that time.

Elizabeth II 1965–1989
(Excluding 1967 Commemorative issue)

The obverse shows a more mature effigy of the Queen to the right, draped and wearing a diamond tiara. ELIZABETH II is curved to the left edge and D • G • REGINA is curved to the right. The reverse is the familiar schooner design used since 1937.

Points of wear: The eyebrow, the hair concealing the top of the ear, the hair at the temple and forehead and the centre of the band of the tiara; also the drapery on the shoulder, particularly the line marking the top of the Queen's gown. On the reverse, the jib, stays, shrouds, the guys between the masts at the top and the line separating the hull from the water.

The coins were struck in silver until 1968 and in nickel beginning in 1968 to date.

EXTREMELY FINE-40

There is slight wear on the eyebrow, the hair covering the top of the ear and the centre of the tiara. There is also slight wear on the lines of drapery on the shoulder, especially the line marking the top of the Queen's gown. On the reverse, there is slight wear on the jib. The rigging and other details are clear and sharp.

ABOUT UNCIRCULATED-50

There are traces of wear on the eyebrow, cheek, hairlines, centre of the tiara and the top line of the drapery. On the reverse, there are traces of wear on the jib.

Elizabeth II 1967

The obverse is the same as described for 1965–1989. To commemorate the centennial of Confederation a different animal motif was used on the reverse of each denomination. The reverse of the ten-cent piece features a mackerel, with 10 CENTS curved to the top and CANADA 1867-1967 curved to the bottom edge of the coin.

Points of wear: On the reverse, the mackerel first shows wear in the middle of the body, followed by the fin back of the gills. The gills are the next to show wear.

Elizabeth II 1990–

The obverse features a contemporary effigy of the Queen, to the right, wearing a necklace, an earring and an elaborate crown. ELIZABETH II is curved to the left edge and D • G • REGINA is curved to the right. The figure is truncated at the base of the neck. The reverse bears the familiar schooner design.

Points of wear: The hair covering the band of the crown near the ear; the hair between the front of the crown and the forehead; and the back of the queen's shoulder where the truncation begins. On the reverse, the jib, the stays and shrouds and the line separating the hull from the water.

SILVER TWENTY AND TWENTY-FIVE CENTS

SILVER TWENTY CENTS
Victoria 1858

The obverse displays a laureate effigy of the Queen to the left, with the hair tied in a chignon or knot at the back, leaving a pendant lock of hair. The hair at the temple is braided, the braid passing around and below the ear to the knot at the back. VICTORIA DEI GRATIA REGINA. with CANADA below. The reverse shows 20 CENTS 1858 in three lines, within a wreath of leaves and surmounted by St. Edward's Crown. Beaded rims.

Points of wear: The eyebrow, the braid of hair below and in front of the ear and the knot of hair at the back. The laurel leaves nearest the ear. On the reverse, the crown and the leaves of the wreath nearest the bow wear first. Convex reverses will wear first at the N of CENTS.

ABOUT GOOD-3

All but the deepest details are gone. On the reverse, the legend is barely legible.

GOOD-4

The braid of hair and the laurel leaves are worn through. The knot of hair at the back is badly worn and the facial features are blurred. On the reverse, no detail remains in either the crown or the leaves of the wreath. The legend is sometimes worn through, especially on convex reverses. Rim beads are indistinct.

VERY GOOD-8

The eyebrow has been worn away and no detail remains in the braid of hair around the ear. The laurel leaves near the ear are worn almost through, the other leaves being considerably worn. There is little detail to the knot of hair at the back. On the reverse, there is little detail remaining in the crown or the wreath. On convex reverses the legend is badly worn.

FINE-12

The eyebrow is indistinct and the segments of the braid begin to run together, those nearest the ear being considerably worn. The laurel leaves are somewhat worn, especially near the ear and the segments of the knot begin to merge. On the reverse, all the leaves of the wreath are worn: the outer third of the top leaves and the outer half of the bottom leaves. The pearls in the arches of the crown begin to merge. The legend shows general wear, the N of CENTS being considerably worn on convex reverses. Rim beads begin to merge.

VERY FINE-20

The eyebrow is considerably worn. The segments of the braid are clear but not sharp, those nearest the ear sometimes beginning to run together. The laurel leaves are clear but not sharp, those nearest the ear sometimes beginning to blur. On the reverse, the wear extends up the sides of the wreath, the outer third or so of the bottom leaves being considerably worn. Other details are clear. Rim beads are clear.

EXTREMELY FINE-40

The eyebrow is worn and the braid is slightly worn, but generally clear and sharp. Laurel leaves are clear and sharp except those nearest the ear which show some wear. On the reverse, the outer edges of the leaves in the wreath show slight wear, especially the bottom leaves. All other details are clear and sharp.

ABOUT UNCIRCULATED-50

There is slight wear on the eyebrow and the laurel leaves nearest the ear. On the reverse, there is slight wear on the bottom leaves of the wreath.

SILVER TWENTY-FIVE CENTS
Victoria 1870–1901

The obverse shows a diademed effigy of the Queen to the left. The Queen's hair is tied in a knot at the back and bound with an ornamental hair band. The hair at the temple is brushed back over the ear and diadem to the knot at the back. Only the ear lobe is visible. Two ribbons hang down from the back, one turning outward and the other inward, overlapping the neck. VICTORIA DEI GRATIA REGINA with CANADA below.

The reverse shows 25 CENTS and the date in three lines within a wreath of maple leaves and surmounted by St. Edward's Crown. Beaded rims.

Points of wear: The eyebrow, the hair over the ear, the knot at the back (especially the bottom half), the jewels of the diadem, the details of the hair band and the end of the ribbon touching the neck. On the reverse, the bottom leaves of the wreath, adjacent to the bow; then the crown begins to wear. A few twenty-five cent pieces in the 1880s have slightly concave reverses. No convex reverses are found. In general, convexity is not pronounced.

ABOUT GOOD-3

Only the deepest details are visible. On the reverse, the legend is often barely legible.

GOOD-4

The hair covering the ear is worn through and no detail remains in the knot of hair at the back. Most of the jewels in the diadem have been worn away. On the reverse, no detail remains in the leaves nor in the crown. The legend is considerably worn. Rim beads are indistinct.

VERY GOOD-8

The eyebrow has been worn away. No detail remains in the hair covering the ear nor in the bottom half of the knot of hair. The jewels in the diadem are partly worn away. On the reverse, there is little detail remaining in the leaves of the wreath and in the crown. The legend is thickened by wear. Rim beads are blurred.

FINE-12

The eyebrow is indistinct. The diadem is clear but the jewels are worn. The hair band is clear. The hair covering the ear and the bottom half of the knot of hair are worn, the strands beginning to run together. The ribbon end touching the neck is indistinct. On the reverse, all the leaves in the wreath are worn, the outer third or so of the top leaves and the outer half or more of the bottom leaves. The pearls in the crown begin to merge into one another. The legend begins to wear. Rim beads begin to merge.

VERY FINE-20

The eyebrow is considerably worn. The hair covering the ear is clear, but not sharp. The knot of hair and the jewels of the diadem are clear while the hair band is sharp. The end of the ribbon touching the neck begins to blur. On the reverse, wear extends up the leaves of the wreath, with the outer third or so of the bottom leaves being worn. The pearls in the arches of the crown are clear but not sharp. Rim beads are clear.

EXTREMELY FINE-40

The eyebrow is worn. The hair covering the ear, the knot of hair, the jewels and hair band are clear and sharp. The ribbon ends are clear. On the reverse, there is slight wear around the edges of the bottom leaves of the wreath and in the crown. Rim beads are clear and sharp.

ABOUT UNCIRCULATED-50

There is slight wear on the eyebrow and on the hair covering the ear. On the reverse, there is slight wear on the bottom leaves of the wreath and on the crown.

Edward VII 1902–1910

The obverse effigy depicts the King to the right, robed and crowned, wearing the chain of the Order of the Garter fastened by a bow on the shoulder. EDWARDVS VII DEI GRATIA REX IMPERATOR

The reverse displays 25 CENTS CANADA and the date, in four lines, within a wreath of maple leaves and surmounted by a stylized Imperial State Crown.

Points of wear: The eyebrow, band of the crown, rim beads, and shoulder bow. On the reverse, the crown and the leaves of the wreath, especially the bottom leaves, are vulnerable. The word CENTS is vulnerable on convex reverses.

ABOUT GOOD-3

All but the deepest details are gone. On the reverse, the legend is barely legible.

GOOD-4

The band of the crown, the bow on the shoulder and the outer rim of the ear are worn through. Little detail remains in the robe, chain, hair and beard. On the reverse, the leaves of the wreath and the crown are badly worn. Rim beads are blurred.

VERY GOOD-8

The eyebrow has been worn away. The band of the crown and the jewels are considerably worn, the band being worn through in the middle. The bow is partly worn through and there is little detail in the robe, hair, beard and chain. On the reverse, the pearls in the arches of the crown are blurred and the central arch is often worn through. There is little detail remaining in the leaves of the wreath. Rim beads are blurred.

FINE-12

The eyebrow is indistinct. The band of the crown, the jewels and the bow are worn. On convex obverses the band of the crown may be worn through. The details of the chain and robe begin to blur. On the reverse, the bottom leaves of the wreath are worn over about half their area, the other leaves over about a third. The central arch of the crown is considerably worn and the pearls in the arches of the crown begin to merge. Rim beads begin to merge.

VERY FINE-20

The eyebrow is considerably worn. The band of the crown, jewels and shoulder bow are clear but not sharp. On the reverse, the bottom leaves of the wreath are worn over the outer third of their area and the central arch of the crown is worn along its entire length. Rim beads are clear.

EXTREMELY FINE-40

The eyebrow is worn and there is slight wear on the shoulder bow and along the band of the crown. Other details are clear and sharp. On the reverse, the bottom leaves of the wreath are only slightly worn while the central arch of the crown shows a spot of wear. Rim beads are clear and sharp.

ABOUT UNCIRCULATED-50

There is slight wear on the eyebrow and on the highest point in the band of the crown. On the reverse, the bottom leaves show slight wear on the edges nearest the rim.

George V 1911–1936

The obverse effigy depicts the King to the left, robed and crowned, wearing the chain of the Order of the Garter fastened by a bow on the shoulder. GEORGIVS V REX ET IND: IMP: in 1911 and GEORGIVS V DEI GRA: REX ET IND: IMP: from 1912 to 1936.

The reverse shows 25 CENTS CANADA and the date in four lines within a wreath of maple leaves and surmounted by a stylized Imperial State Crown.

Points of wear: The eyebrow, band of the crown and the shoulder bow. On the reverse, the leaves in the wreath, especially at the bottom, are vulnerable. The word CENTS is vulnerable on convex reverses.

ABOUT GOOD-3

All but the deepest details are gone. On the reverse, the legend is barely legible.

GOOD-4

The band of the crown and the bow are worn through and there is little detail in the robe. On the reverse, the leaves of the wreath show very little detail. The legend on convex reverses is badly worn. Rim beads are blurred.

VERY GOOD-8

The eyebrow has been worn away. The band of the crown and the jewels are considerably worn, being worn through in the middle. The shoulder bow is considerably worn while the robe shows little detail. On the reverse, the pearls in the arches of the crown are blurred and the central arch is often worn through. Little detail remains in the leaves of the wreath. The word CENTS may be worn through at the N on convex reverses. Rim beads are blurred.

FINE-12

The eyebrow is indistinct. The band of the crown, jewels and shoulder bow are worn. The details of the chain and robe begin to blur. On the reverse, the bottom leaves of the wreath are worn over about half their area, the other leaves over about a third. The central arch of the crown is considerably worn and the pearls in the arches begin to merge. Rim beads begin to merge.

VERY FINE-20

The eyebrow is considerably worn. The band of the crown, jewels and shoulder bow are all clear but not sharp. On the reverse, the outer third of the bottom leaves of the wreath are worn and the central arch of the crown is worn along its entire length. Rim beads are clear.

EXTREMELY FINE-40

The eyebrow is worn and there is slight wear along the band of the crown. Other details remain clear and sharp. On the reverse, the bottom leaves of the wreath are only slightly worn and the central arch of the crown shows a spot of wear. Rim beads are clear and sharp.

ABOUT UNCIRCULATED-50

There is slight wear on the eyebrow and the centre of the band of the crown. On the reverse, there is slight wear in the centre of the band of the crown.

THE DOTTED 1936 TWENTY-FIVE CENTS

The dotted 1936 reverse is convex in such a way that the CAN of CANADA is especially vulnerable to wear. Note that the dot—about the size of one of the pearls in the arches of the crown—because of its secure position at the bottom of the coin between the ends of the ribbon which ties the wreath, remains visible even after the date has worn away.

GOOD-4

CAN is worn off; ADA is indistinct.

VERY GOOD-8

CANADA is blurred; CAN is almost worn away—BUT MUST BE LEGIBLE.

FINE-12

All of CANADA is considerably worn, with CAN badly thickened.

VERY FINE-20

CAN is worn and ADA begins to wear.

EXTREMELY FINE-40

CAN is slightly worn. Other details are clear and sharp.

ABOUT UNCIRCULATED-50

There are very slight traces of wear on CAN.

George VI 1937–1952

The obverse features the King, bare-headed, to the left. The effigy is truncated at the base of the neck. GEORGIVS VI D : G : REX ET IND : IMP: from 1937 to 1947 and GEORGIVS VI DEI GRATIA REX from 1948 to 1952. On the reverse is depicted the head of a caribou to the left, with 25 CENTS in two lines between the antlers. • CANADA • is curved to the left edge, with • and the date curved to the right edge. Beaded rims.

Points of wear: The eyebrow and ear lobe, the hair above the ear and the hairline at the temple and at the back of the neck. On the reverse, the first place to show wear is the head of the caribou between the eye and the ear and extending toward the snout. The hair on the throat also shows early wear.

VERY GOOD-8

Little detail remains in the hair and the rim of the ear. The facial features begin to coarsen. On the reverse, there is little detail to the head of the caribou. The hair on the throat is blurred and the antlers are considerably worn. 25 CENTS and the date are considerably thickened by wear.

FINE-12

The eyebrow has been worn away and there is little detail in the hair above the ear. The hairline at the temple and the back of the neck is indistinct. The ear is considerably worn. On the reverse, there is little detail between the caribou's eye and ear and the rest of the head is considerably worn. The hair at the throat begins to blur and the antlers begin to thicken. Rim beads begin to merge.

VERY FINE-20

The eyebrow is indistinct and the hair above the ear is considerably worn. The hairline at the temple and the back of the neck is rather blurred and the outer rim of the ear shows wear up from the lobe. On the reverse, wear on the caribou's head extends along the antlers and snout. The ear of the caribou shows considerable wear while the hair at the throat is clear. Rim beads are clear.

EXTREMELY FINE-40

The eyebrow is worn and there is slight wear on the hair at the temple and above the ear, with a spot of wear on the ear lobe. On the reverse, the head of the caribou shows slight wear around the eye and at the base of the ear. The hair at the throat is clear and sharp. Rim beads are clear and sharp.

ABOUT UNCIRCULATED-50

There is slight wear on the eyebrow and the ear lobe. On the reverse, there are traces of wear around the eye of the caribou and at the base of the ear.

Elizabeth II 1953–1964

The obverse features a draped, laureate effigy of the Queen to the right. ELIZABETH II DEI GRATIA REGINA

The reverse shows the head of a caribou as for the previous reign, with 25 CENTS in two lines between the antlers, • CANADA • is curved to the left edge while • and the date are curved to the right. Beaded rims.

Points of wear: The eyebrow, the middle leaves of the laurel wreath, the hair about the ear and the lines of drapery over the shoulder. On the reverse, wear occurs on the area between the eye and ear of the caribou, extending toward the snout and the hair on the throat.

FINE-12

The eyebrow has been worn away and the laurel wreath is worn almost through. The shoulder drapery is indistinct. On the reverse, there is little detail between the ear and eye of the caribou. The rest of the caribou's head is considerably worn. The hair at the throat begins to blur and the antlers begin to thicken. Rim beads begin to merge.

VERY FINE-20

The eyebrow is considerably worn. The laurel wreath is worn and the wear on the hair above the ear extends toward the forehead. The lines of drapery are clear. On the reverse, wear on the head of the caribou extends along the antlers and snout, while the ear is considerably worn. The hair at the throat is clear. Rim beads are clear.

EXTREMELY FINE-40

The eyebrow is worn and there is slight wear on the hair and laurel leaves above the ear. The lines of drapery are clear and sharp. On the reverse, the head of the caribou shows slight wear around the eye and at the base of the ear. The hair at the throat is clear and sharp. Rim beads are clear and sharp.

ABOUT UNCIRCULATED-50

There is slight wear on the eyebrow. On the reverse, there are traces of wear around the caribou's eye and at the base of the ear. Rim beads are clear and sharp.

SILVER AND NICKEL TWENTY-FIVE CENTS

The mint continued to strike twenty-five cent pieces in .800 silver until mid-1967 when the composition was changed to .500 silver. During 1968 the composition was changed to nickel.

Elizabeth II 1965–1989
(Excluding commemorative issues)

The obverse shows a more mature effigy of the Queen to the right, draped and wearing a diamond tiara. ELIZABETH II is curved to the left edge and D • G • REGINA is curved to the right. The reverse is the familiar caribou design used since 1937.

Points of wear: The eyebrow, the hair concealing the top of the ear, the hair at the temple and forehead and the centre of the band of the tiara; also the drapery on the shoulder, particularly the line marking the top of the Queen's gown. On the reverse, wear occurs on the area between the eye and ear of the caribou, extending toward the snout and the hair on the throat.

EXTREMELY FINE-40

There is slight wear on the eyebrow, the hair covering the top of the ear and the centre of the tiara. There is also slight wear on the lines of drapery on the shoulder, especially the line marking the top of the Queen's gown. On the reverse, the caribou's head shows slight wear around the eye and at the base of the ear. Other details are clear and sharp.

ABOUT UNCIRCULATED-50

There is slight wear on the eyebrow. On the reverse, there are traces of wear around the caribou's eye and at the base of the ear. Rim beads are clear and sharp.

Elizabeth II 1967

The obverse is the same as described for 1965–1989. To commemorate the centennial of Confederation a different animal motif was used on the reverse of each denomination. The reverse of the twenty-five cent piece features a bobcat, with 25 CENTS curved to the top and CANADA 1867-1967 curved to the bottom edge of the coin.

Points of wear: On the reverse, wear occurs first on the bobcat's foreleg directly below its head. The whiskers about the jaw and then the shoulder are the next to show wear.

Elizabeth II 1973

The obverse is the same as described for 1965–1989. In 1973, to commemorate the centenary of the Royal Canadian Mounted Police, the reverse of the twenty-five cent piece features a Mountie on horseback.

Points of wear: On the reverse, the shoulder of the mountie is the first place to show wear, then his knee. Later the face of the mountie and the rear of the horse will show wear.

Elizabeth II 1990 to date
(Excluding commemorative issues)

The obverse features a contemporary crowned effigy of the Queen, to the right, wearing a necklace and earring. ELIZABETH II is curved to the left edge and D • G • REGINA is curved to the right. The reverse bears the familiar caribou design.

Points of wear: The cheek, earring and the hair covering the ear. On the reverse, wear occurs on the area between the eye and ear of the caribou, extending toward the snout and the hair on the throat.

Elizabeth II 1992

The common obverse shows the crowned effigy of the Queen to the right, wearing a necklace and earrings, with ELIZABETH II curved to the left edge and D • G • REGINA curved to the right. CANADA is curved to the top and 1867–1992 to the bottom.

To celebrate the 125th anniversary of Confederation, twenty-five cent pieces were struck with twelve different reverse designs, each bearing the name of a province or territory in its bilingual inscription with 25 CENTS curved to the bottom edge. Each design depicts a scene from a different province or territory.

Common Obverse

Points of wear: On the common obverse, the cheek, the earring and the hair covering the ear are the first points to show wear.

Alberta
Hoodoos

British Columbia
Natural Beauty of British Columbia

Manitoba
Lower Fort Garry

New Brunswick
Covered Bridge at Newton, NB

Newfoundland
Fisherman in Grandy Dory

Northwest Territories
Prehistoric Inuit "Inukshuk"

Nova Scotia
Lighthouse at Peggy's Cove

Ontario
Jack Pines

Prince Edward Island
Cousins Shore

Quebec
Percé Rock

Saskatchewan
Prairie Symbols

Yukon
Kaskawalsh Glacier

SILVER FIFTY CENTS

Victoria 1870–1901

The obverse shows a diademed effigy of the Queen to the left, with the hair tied in a knot or chignon at the back and bound with an ornamental hair band. The hair at the temple is brushed back over the ear and diadem to the knot at the back. Only the ear lobe is visible. Two ribbon ends hang down from the back, one turning outward and the other inward, overlapping the neck. VICTORIA DEI GRATIA REGINA with CANADA below.

The reverse shows 50 CENTS and the date in three lines within a wreath of maple leaves and surmounted by St. Edward's Crown. Beaded rims.

Points of wear: The eyebrow, the hair over the ear, the knot at the back (especially the bottom half), the jewels of the diadem, the details of the hair band and the end of the ribbon touching the neck. On the reverse, the leaves of the wreath adjacent to the bow at the bottom will show wear first. The wear then extends upward towards the crown. Most fifty-cent pieces have slightly concave reverses.

ABOUT GOOD-3

Only the deepest details are visible. On the reverse, the legend is often barely legible.

GOOD-4

The hair covering the top of the ear is worn through and there is no detail in the knot of hair at the back. Most of the jewels in the diadem have been worn off. On the reverse, the leaves of the wreath show virtually no detail and the crown is badly worn. The legend is thickened by wear. Rim beads are indistinct.

VERY GOOD-8

The eyebrow has been worn away and there is no detail in the hair covering the top of the ear. There is no detail in the bottom half of the knot at the back. The jewels in the diadem are partly worn away. On the reverse, there is little detail in the crown or the leaves in the wreath. Legends are somewhat thickened by wear. Rim beads are blurred.

FINE-12

The eyebrow is indistinct. The diadem is clear but the jewels are worn. The hair band is clear. The hair covering the top of the ear and in the bottom half of the knot is worn, the strands beginning to merge. The ribbon end touching the neck is indistinct. On the reverse, all the leaves of the wreath are worn, the outer half or more of the bottom leaves and the outer third or so of the top leaves. The pearls in the arches of the crown begin to merge. The legends begin to show signs of wear. Rim beads begin to merge.

VERY FINE-20

The eyebrow is considerably worn. The hair covering the top of the ear and in the knot at the back are clear but not sharp. The jewels of the diadem are clear but not sharp, while the hair band remains clear and sharp. The ribbon end touching the neck begins to blur. On the reverse, wear extends up the wreath, the outer third or so of the bottom leaves being worn. The pearls in the arches of the crown are clear. Rim beads are clear.

EXTREMELY FINE-40

The eyebrow is worn. The hair covering the top of the ear, the knot at the back, the jewels and hair band are clear and sharp. On the reverse, there is slight wear around the edges of the bottom leaves and on the crown. Rim beads are clear and sharp.

ABOUT UNCIRCULATED-50

There is slight wear on the eyebrow and the hair covering the top of the ear. The ribbon ends are clear. On the reverse, there is slight wear on the crown and around the edges of the bottom leaves of the wreath.

Edward VII 1902–1910

The obverse features a crowned, robed effigy of the King to the right, with the chain of the Order of the Garter fastened by a large bow on the shoulder. EDWARDVS VII DEI GRATIA REX IMPERATOR.

The reverse shows 50 CENTS CANADA and the date in four lines within a wreath of maple leaves and surmounted by a stylized Imperial State Crown. Beaded rims.

The reverses are slightly convex on 1902, 1903 and 1906 issues and slightly concave on 1904 and 1905 issues. Other dates are flat.

Points of wear: The eyebrow, band of the crown, shoulder bow, ear and beard. On concave reverses, the crown and the bottom leaves of the wreath wear first and on convex reverses the N in CENTS is the earliest point to wear..

ABOUT GOOD-3

All but the deepest details are gone. On the reverse the legend is barely legible.

GOOD-4

The band of the crown, the bow and the outer rim of the ear are worn through. Little detail remains on the robe, chain, hair and beard. On the reverse, the leaves of the wreath and the crown are badly worn. Rim beads are blurred.

VERY GOOD-8

The eyebrow has been worn away and the band of the crown is worn through in the middle. The shoulder bow is partly worn through and the hair and beard show little detail. The outline of the ear is indistinct. On the reverse, the pearls in the arches of the crown are blurred and the central arch is often worn through. The leaves of the wreath show little detail. Rim beads are blurred.

FINE-12

The eyebrow is indistinct. The band of the crown and the jewels are considerably worn. The shoulder bow is worn. On convex obverses the band of the crown is sometimes worn through at its highest point. On the reverse, the pearls in the arches of the crown begin to merge, and the central arch is considerably worn. The bottom leaves of the wreath are worn to the extent of about half their area and the other leaves to about a third. Rim beads begin to merge.

VERY FINE-20

The eyebrow is considerably worn. The band and jewels of the crown are clear but not sharp. On the reverse, the bottom leaves of the wreath are worn over the outer third or so of their area and the central arch of the crown shows wear along its entire length. Rim beads are clear.

EXTREMELY FINE-40

The eyebrow is worn while there is slight wear on the band of the crown and the shoulder bow. Other details remain clear and sharp. On the reverse, the bottom leaves of the wreath show slight wear along the edges adjacent to the rim and the central arch of the crown shows a spot of wear. Rim beads are clear and sharp.

ABOUT UNCIRCULATED-50

There is slight wear on the eyebrow and on the highest point in the band of the crown. On the reverse, the bottom leaves of the wreath have very slight wear along the edges adjacent to the rim.

George V 1911–1936

The obverse shows a robed, crowned effigy of the King to the left, wearing the chain of the Order of the Garter fastened by a bow on the shoulder. GEORGIVS V REX ET IND: IMP: in 1911; GEORGIVS V DEI GRA: REX ET IND: IMP: from 1912 to 1936.

The reverse shows 50 CENTS CANADA and the date in four lines within a wreath of maple leaves and surmounted by a stylized Imperial State Crown. Beaded rims.

Points of wear: The eyebrow, the band of the crown and the shoulder bow. On the reverse, the leaves of the wreath are vulnerable, especially at the bottom. The crown also wears early. On convex reverses CENTS is the first element to wear. Some coins of the 1931, 1932, 1934 and 1936 issues have slightly convex reverses.

ABOUT GOOD-3

All but the deepest details are gone. On the reverse, the legend is barely legible.

GOOD-4

The band of the crown and the shoulder bow are worn through and there is little detail in the robe. On the reverse, there is little detail to the wreath and on convex reverses the legend is badly worn. Rim beads are blurred.

VERY GOOD-8

The eyebrow has been worn away. The band and jewels of the crown and the shoulder bow are considerably worn, the band of the crown being worn through in the middle. There is little detail to the robe. On the reverse, the pearls in the arches of the crown are blurred and the central arch is often worn through. The leaves of the wreath show little detail. On convex reverses the N of CENTS may be worn through. Rim beads are blurred.

FINE-12

The eyebrow is indistinct. The shoulder bow and the band and jewels of the crown are worn. The details of the robe and chain begin to blur. On the reverse, the outer half of the bottom leaves and the outer third or so of the other leaves of the wreath are worn. The central arch of the crown is considerably worn and the pearls in the arches of the crown begin to merge. Rim beads begin to merge.

VERY FINE-20

The eyebrow is considerably worn. The band of the crown, its jewels and the shoulder bow are clear but not sharp. On the reverse, the outer third or so of the bottom leaves of the wreath are worn. The central arch of the crown is worn along its entire length. Rim beads are clear.

EXTREMELY FINE-40

The eyebrow is worn and there is slight wear along the band of the crown. Other details remain clear and sharp. On the reverse, the bottom leaves of the wreath are worn along the edges adjacent to the rim and the central arch of the crown shows a spot of wear. Rim beads are clear and sharp.

ABOUT UNCIRCULATED-50

There is slight wear on the eyebrow and the centre of the band of the crown. On the reverse, there is slight wear on the central arch of the crown and along the edges of the bottom leaves of the wreath.

George VI 1937–1952

The obverse features a bare-headed effigy of the King to the left. The effigy is truncated at the base of the neck. GEORGIVS VI D : G : REX ET IND : IMP: from 1937 to 1947 and GEORGIVS VI DEI GRATIA REX from 1948 to 1952.

The reverse bears a crowned shield of the arms of the Dominion of Canada, with a lion on the left holding a Union Jack and a unicorn on the right holding a fleur de lys flag. The whole design rests on a base of clouds. 50 CENTS is above and CANADA • and the date are curved to the bottom edge. Beaded rims.

Points of wear: The eyebrow and ear lobe; the hair above the ear and the hairline at the temple and at the back of the neck. On the reverse, the first portion to wear is the top of the shield, especially at the left. Wear then spreads to the base of the crown.

VERY GOOD-8

There is little detail in the hair or the rim of the ear. The facial features begin to coarsen. On the reverse, the top left corner of the shield is worn through in some cases. The entire shield is considerably thickened and coarsened by wear. The forelegs of the lion and unicorn are badly worn.

FINE-12

The eyebrow has been worn away and there is little detail to the hair above the ear. The hairline at the temple and the back of the neck is indistinct. The ear is considerably worn. On the reverse, there is considerable wear over the bottom of the crown and the top third of the shield, the heaviest wear being at the top left corner of the shield. The lines dividing the lower two thirds of the shield are thickened and the forelegs of the lion and the unicorn are worn. Rim beads begin to merge.

VERY FINE-20

The eyebrow is indistinct and the hair above the ear is considerably worn. The hairline is rather blurred at the temple and the back of the neck. The outer rim of the ear shows wear up from the lobe. On the reverse, wear extends into the English and Scottish arms in the shield and up toward the central cross of the crown. Other details are clear.

EXTREMELY FINE-40

The eyebrow is worn and there is slight wear in the hair at the temple and above the ear, with a spot of wear on the ear lobe. On the reverse, there is slight thickening of the top of the shield and the base of the crown. Other details are clear and sharp.

ABOUT UNCIRCULATED-50

There is slight wear on the eyebrow, the hair above the ear and the ear lobe. On the reverse, there is slight wear at the top of the shield.

Elizabeth II 1953–1958

The obverse shows a draped, laureate effigy of the Queen to the right. ELIZABETH II DEI GRATIA REGINA

The reverse bears the crowned shield of the arms of the Dominion of Canada, supported by lion and unicorn, as in the previous reign. The inscriptions are as described for the previous reign. In 1955 the reverse was redesigned to make the shield smaller. Beaded rims.

Points of wear: The middle leaves of the laurel wreath, the eyebrow, the hair over the ear and the lines of drapery over the shoulder. On the reverse, the top of the shield wears first, especially at the top left corner. Wear then spreads to the base of the crown.

FINE-12

The eyebrow has been worn away and the laurel leaves are worn almost through. The shoulder drapery is indistinct. On the reverse, there is considerable wear over the bottom of the crown and the top third of the shield, the heaviest wear being at the top left corner of the shield. The lines dividing the lower two thirds of the shield are thickened and the forelegs of the lion and unicorn are worn. Rim beads begin to merge.

VERY FINE-20

The eyebrow is considerably worn. The laurel leaves are worn and wear on the hair above the ear extends toward the forehead. The lines of the drapery are clear. On the reverse, wear extends into the English and Scottish arms of the shield and up toward the central cross of the the crown. Other details are clear.

EXTREMELY FINE-40

The eyebrow is worn and there is slight wear on the laurel leaves above the ear. The drapery and other details are clear and sharp. On the reverse, there is a slight thickening of the top of the shield and the base of the crown. Other details are clear and sharp.

ABOUT UNCIRCULATED-50

There is slight wear on the eyebrow. On the reverse, there is slight wear at the top of the shield.

Elizabeth II 1959–1964

The obverse is the same as described for the issues from 1953 to 1958.

The reverse displays a new treatment of the coat of arms. The shield is spade-shaped and is surmounted by a visored helmet with plumes. A lion holding a maple leaf stands atop the helmet. The shield is supported on the left by a lion holding a Union Jack and on the right by a unicorn holding a fleur de lys flag. The shield and its supporters rest on a ribbon inscribed A MARI USQUE AD MARE. A crown, dividing the date, is at the top. CANADA is curved at the left and 50 CENTS at the right and sprays of heraldic flowers occupy the space below the ribbon. Beaded rims.

The issues of 1959 and 1962 have remarkably convex obverses. This condition, combined with the relatively low relief of the effigy, leads to more rapid wear of the obverse than usual.

Points of wear: The middle leaves of the laurel wreath, the eyebrow, the hair over the ear and the lines of drapery over the shoulder. On the reverse, the chief points of wear are the crown, the front of the helmet and the forelegs of the shield's supporters.

VERY FINE-20

The eyebrow is considerably worn. The laurel wreath is worn. Wear on the hair over the ear extends to the forehead. The lines of the drapery are clear. On the reverse, the centre of the crown is worn, the forelegs of the supporters are thickened. A spot of wear is on the helmet.

EXTREMELY FINE-40

The eyebrow is worn and there is slight wear on the laurel leaves and on the hair above the ear. Other details remain clear and sharp. On the reverse, the crown shows a spot of wear and the forelegs of the supporters are slightly worn. Other details are clear and sharp.

ABOUT UNCIRCULATED-50

There is slight wear on the eyebrow. On the reverse, there is slight wear on the crown and the forelegs of the supporters.

SILVER AND NICKEL FIFTY CENTS

The coins were struck in silver until 1967. In 1968 the size of the coin was reduced, and all issues from 1968 have been struck in nickel. Both the obverse and reverse devices were reduced in size in 1977 and the denticles were replaced by a beaded border moved in from the rim. Minor modifications to the devices were made in other years, but do not affect the sequence of wear on the coins.

Elizabeth II 1965–1989
(Excluding 1967 commemorative issue)

The obverse displays a more mature effigy of the Queen to the right, draped and wearing a diamond tiara. ELIZABETH II is curved to the left edge and D • G • REGINA is curved to the right.

The reverse shows the new arms as described for the issues from 1959 to 1964.

Points of wear: The eyebrow, the hair concealing the top of the ear, the hair at the temple and forehead and the centre of the band of the tiara. The drapery over the shoulder, particularly the line marking the top of the Queen's gown. On the reverse, the crown, the front of the helmet and the forelegs of the supporters will wear first.

EXTREMELY FINE-40

The eyebrow is worn and there is slight wear on the hair concealing the top of the ear. The drapery and other details are clear and sharp. On the reverse, the crown shows a spot of wear and the forelegs of the supporters are slightly worn. Other details are clear and sharp.

ABOUT UNCIRCULATED-50

There is slight wear on the eyebrow. On the reverse, there is slight wear on the crown and on the forelegs of the supporters.

Elizabeth II 1967

The obverse is the same as described for 1965–1989. To commemorate the centennial of Confederation a different animal motif was used on the reverse of each denomination. The reverse of the fifty-cent piece features a howling wolf.

Points of wear: On the reverse, the wolf's ear will show wear first, followed by the middle of the haunch. Later, wear shows on the cheek and shoulders and spreads as the wear progresses.

Elizabeth II 1990–

The obverse features a contemporary crowned effigy of the Queen, to the right, wearing a necklace and earring. ELIZABETH II is curved to the left edge and D • G • REGINA is curved to the right.

The reverse bears the same design of the National Arms of Canada as used on the issues of 1965–1989.

Points of wear: The cheek, the earring and the hair covering the ear. On the reverse, the crown, the front of the helmet and the forelegs of the supporters will wear first.

SILVER DOLLARS

George V 1935, 1936

The obverse shows a robed, crowned effigy of the King to the left, wearing the chain of the Order of the Garter fastened by a bow on the shoulder. GEORGIVS V REX IMPERATOR ANNO REGNI XXV in 1935, with the effigy carried full to the bottom edge and GEORGIVS V DEI GRA: REX ET IND: IMP: in 1936, with the effigy truncated as the other coins of the reign.

The reverse shows a canoe, to the right, loaded with provisions and manned by a native guide and a voyageur. Behind the canoe is an islet with two trees. The field above the islet is filled with incuse lines representing the Northern Lights. CANADA is curved to the top edge and DOLLAR is curved to the bottom. The date appears in the exergue below the canoe.

Points of wear: The eyebrow, the band of the crown and the shoulder bow. The details of the robe and chain are next to show wear.. On the reverse, the centre of the canoe is the first point to wear. The backs of the men in the canoe are also significant points of wear.

VERY GOOD-8

The eyebrow has been worn away. The band and jewels of the crown and the shoulder bow are considerably worn. The robe and chain show little detail. On the reverse, the men and trees are considerably worn and little detail remains in the canoe. The Northern Lights are faint.

FINE-12

The eyebrow is indistinct. The band and jewels of the crown and the shoulder bow are worn. The details of the robe and chain begin to blur. On the reverse, the canoe is considerably worn and the men and trees show wear. The bodies of the men are thickened by wear. Rim beads begin to merge.

VERY FINE-20

The eyebrow is considerably worn. The band and jewels of the crown and the shoulder bow are clear but not sharp. On the reverse, the wear spreads to the pack in the centre of the canoe and the details of the hull are indistinct. There is slight wear on the bodies of the men.

EXTREMELY FINE-40

The eyebrow is worn. The band and jewels of the crown show slight wear. Other details are clear and sharp. On the reverse, there is slight wear at the centre of the canoe.

ABOUT UNCIRCULATED-50

There is slight wear on the eyebrow and very slight wear in the centre of the band of the crown. On the reverse, there is very slight wear on the upper center of the canoe.

George VI 1937–1952
(Excluding commemorative issues)

The obverse features a bare-headed effigy of the King to the left. GEORGIVS VI D : G : REX
ET IND : IMP: from 1937 to 1947 and GEORGIVS VI DEI GRATIA REX from 1948 to 1952.
    The reverse shows the familiar voyageur design of the previous reign.

Points of wear: The eyebrow, the ear lobe, the hair above the ear and the hairline at the temple
and at the back of the neck. On the reverse, wear begins at the centre of the canoe and along
the backs of the men.

VERY GOOD-8

There is little detail to the hair or the rim of the ear. The facial features begin to coarsen. On
the reverse, the men and trees are considerably worn while the canoe shows little detail. The
Northern Lights are rather faint.

FINE-12

The eyebrow has been worn away and little detail remains in the hair above the ear. The
hairline is indistinct at the temple and the back of the neck. The ear is considerably worn. On
the reverse, the canoe is considerably worn. The men and trees show wear, the bodies of the
men being thickened.

VERY FINE-20

The eyebrow is indistinct. The hair above the ear is considerably worn. The outer rim of the ear shows wear up from the lobe. The hairline is rather blurred at the temple and the back of the neck. On the reverse, wear spreads to the pack in the centre of the canoe and the details of the hull are indistinct. Slight wear is evident on the bodies of the men.

EXTREMELY FINE-40

The eyebrow is worn and there is slight wear in the hair above the ear and in the hairline at the temple and at the back of the neck, with a spot of wear on the ear lobe. On the reverse, there is slight wear at the centre of the canoe. Other details remain clear and sharp.

ABOUT UNCIRCULATED-50

There is slight wear on the eyebrow and the ear lobe. On the reverse, there is very slight wear on the upper middle of the canoe.

George VI 1939

The obverse is the same as described for 1937–1952. The reverse shows the centre block of the Dominion Parliament Buildings at Ottawa. FIDE SVORVM REGNAT (By the faith of his people he reigns) is curved to the top edge. CANADA and the date appear in two lines in the exergue and 1 DOLLAR is curved to the bottom edge.

Points of wear: The eyebrow, the ear lobe, the hair above the ear and the hairline at the temple and at the back of the neck. On the reverse, the first place to wear is the doorway to the Peace Tower. The ground and the butresses near the ends of the building wear next.

VERY GOOD-8

There is little detail to the hair and the rim of the ear. Facial features begin to coarsen. On the reverse, part of the tower outline has been worn away and there is little detail to the rest of the building.

FINE-12

The eyebrow has been worn away and there is little detail to the hair above the ear. The hairline is indistinct at the temple and at the back of the neck. The ear shows considerable wear. On the reverse, the tower is considerably worn and the rest of the building begins to blur. Rim beads begin to merge.

VERY FINE-20

The eyebrow is indistinct and the hair above the ear is considerably worn. The outer rim of the ear shows wear extending upward from the lobe. The hairline is rather blurred at the temple and at the back of the neck. On the reverse, wear begins to extend up the tower. The windows and the outlines of the butresses and tower are clear but no longer sharp. Rim beads are clear.

EXTREMELY FINE-40

The eyebrow is worn and there is slight wear on the hair above the ear and on the hairline at the temple and at the back of the neck. On the reverse, slight wear shows at the doorway. Other details are clear and sharp.

ABOUT UNCIRCULATED-50

There is slight wear on the eyebrow and very slight wear on the ear lobe and on the hairline at the temple. On the reverse, there is slight wear at the doorway.

George VI 1949

The obverse is the same as described for 1937–1952. The reverse shows John Cabot's ship, the *Matthew,* sailing left. Below the water, between two horizontal lines, is the motto FLOREAT TERRA NOVA (May Newfoundland Flourish). CANADA is curved to the top edge and DOLLAR is curved to the bottom. 1949 appears in the exergue, below the motto. Beaded rims. This coin has a high relief.

Points of wear: The eyebrow, the ear lobe, the hair above the ear and the hairline at the temple and at the back of the neck. On the reverse, the mainsails and main shrouds and the Latin motto are most susceptible to wear.

FINE-12

The eyebrow has been worn away and there is little detail to the hair above the ear. The hairline at the temple and the back of the neck is indistinct and the ear shows considerable wear. On the reverse, the mainsails and shrouds are considerably worn while the other rigging is clear. The Latin motto is slightly worn.

VERY FINE-20

The eyebrow is indistinct. The hair above the ear is considerably worn and the outer rim of the ear shows wear extending up from the lobe. The hairline at the temple and at the back of the neck is rather blurred. On the reverse, wear extends upward along the shrouds from the hull into the centre of the mainsails. The Latin motto and other details are clear and sharp.

EXTREMELY FINE-40

The eyebrow is worn and there is slight wear on the hair above the ear and the hairline at the temple, with a spot of wear on the ear lobe. On the reverse, there is slight wear on the mainsails and shrouds immediately above the hull.

ABOUT UNCIRCULATED-50

There is slight wear on the eyebrow, on the hairline at the temple and on the ear lobe. On the reverse, there is very slight wear on the mainsails and shrouds immediately above the hull.

Elizabeth II 1953–1963
(Excluding commemorative issues)

The obverse shows a draped laureate effigy of the Queen to the right. ELIZABETH II DEI GRATIA REGINA

The reverse shows the familiar voyageur design introduced in 1935.

Points of wear: The middle leaves of the laurel wreath, the eyebrow, the hair over the ear and the lines of the drapery over the shoulder. On the reverse, wear begins at the centre of the canoe and along the bodies of the men in the canoe.

FINE-12

The eyebrow has been worn away and the laurel wreath is worn almost through. The shoulder drapery is indistinct. On the reverse, the canoe is considerably worn and the trees show wear. The bodies of the men are thickened by wear. Rim beads begin to merge.

VERY FINE-20

The eyebrow is considerably worn. The laurel wreath is worn and the wear on the hair over the ear extends to the forehead. The lines of drapery are clear. On the reverse, wear spreads to the pack in the centre of the canoe and the details of the hull are indistinct. There is slight wear on the bodies of the men.

EXTREMELY FINE-40

The eyebrow is worn and there is slight wear on the laurel leaves above the ear. Other details are clear and sharp. On the reverse, there is slight wear at the centre of the canoe. Other details remain clear and sharp.

ABOUT UNCIRCULATED-50

There is slight wear on the eyebrow. On the reverse, there is very slight wear on the upper middle of the canoe.

Elizabeth II 1958

The obverse is the same as described for 1953–1963. The reverse depicts a large totem pole against a background of distant mountains. The dates 1858 and 1958 are shown in two lines to the left of the totem, above the mountains. CANADA is curved to the upper left edge and BRITISH COLUMBIA is curved to the right, with DOLLAR appearing in the exergue.

Points of wear: The eyebrow, the middle leaves of the laurel wreath, the hair over the ear and the lines of the drapery over the shoulder. On the reverse, the nose on the top face of the totem is the first part of the design to show wear.

EXTREMELY FINE-40

The eyebrow is worn and there is slight wear on the laurel leaves and on the hair over the ear. Other details are clear and sharp. On the reverse, there is slight wear along the nose of the top face on the totem. Other details are clear and sharp.

ABOUT UNCIRCULATED-50

There is slight wear on the eyebrow. On the reverse, there is very slight wear on the nose of the top face on the totem.

Elizabeth II 1964

The obverse is the same as described for 1953–1964. The reverse features the stylized heraldic flowers of England, Ireland, Scotland and France arranged in a small cross within a small circle enclosed by • CHARLOTTETOWN • curved to the top outside of the circle and QUEBEC curved to the bottom outside of the circle. Curved to the border of the coin are CANADA at the top and DOLLAR at the bottom, with 1864 to the left and 1964 to the right.

Points of wear: The eyebrow, the middle leaves of the laurel wreath, the hair over the ear and the lines of the drapery over the shoulder. On the reverse, the flowers in the centre are the first parts of the design to show wear.

EXTREMELY FINE-40

The eyebrow is worn and there is slight wear on the laurel leaves above the ear. Other details are clear and sharp. On the reverse, there is wear on the flowers at the centre of the coin.

ABOUT UNCIRCULATED-50

There is slight wear on the eyebrow. On the reverse, there is slight wear on the flowers at the centre of the coin.

Elizabeth II 1965, 1966

The obverse displays a more mature effigy of the Queen to the right, draped and wearing a diamond tiara. ELIZABETH II is curved to the left edge and D • G • REGINA is curved to the right.

The reverse features the familiar voyageur design used since 1935.

Points of wear: The eyebrow, the hair concealing the top of the ear, the hair at the temple and forehead and the centre of the band of the tiara; also the drapery over the shoulder, especially the line marking the top of the queen's gown. On the reverse, the centre of the canoe and the bodies of the men are the first features to show wear.

EXTREMELY FINE-40

The eyebrow is worn and there is slight wear on the hair covering the ear and the centre of the tiara. The drapery over the shoulder shows slight wear along the line marking the top of the Queen's gown. On the reverse, there is slight wear at the centre of the canoe. Other details are clear and sharp.

ABOUT UNCIRCULATED-50

There is a trace of wear on the eyebrow. On the reverse, there is slight wear at the upper centre of the canoe.

Elizabeth II 1967

The obverse is the same as described for 1965, 1966. To commemorate the centennial of Confederation a different animal motif was used on the reverse of each denomination. The reverse of the dollar features a Canada Goose, flying to the left.

Points of wear: On the reverse, the head of the Canada Goose shows wear first. Then wear occurs on the central area of the wing and spreads upwards towards the body. Later, the middle area of the neck begins to wear.

NICKEL DOLLARS

Elizabeth II 1968–1986

(Excluding commemorative issues)

The obverse and reverse are the same designs as the 1965, 1966 issues, but the size is greatly reduced and the composition has been changed to nickel. In 1972 the obverse beads were moved away from the rim and the effigy was reduced in size. In 1977, the obverse and reverse devices and the legends were reduced in size, the legends being placed farther from the rim. In 1978 both sides of the dollar were modified to appear more like the issues prior to 1977.

Points of wear: The eyebrow, the hair concealing the top of the ear, the hair at the temple and forehead and the centre of the band of the tiara; also the drapery over the shoulder, especially the line marking the top of the queen's gown. On the reverse, the centre of the canoe and the bodies of the men are the first features to show wear.

Elizabeth II 1970

The obverse is the same as described for 1968–1986. For the centennial of Manitoba's entry into Confederation the reverse design depicts the prairie crocus, with MANITOBA and the dates 1870 • 1970 curved to the top edge and separated by a small maple leaf. CANADA and DOLLAR are curved to the bottom edge, also separated by a small maple leaf.

Elizabeth II 1971

The obverse is the same as described for 1968–1986. To celebrate the centennial of British Columbia's entry into Confederation the reverse design depicts the provincial flower (the flowering dogwood) protruding above the provincial arms from behind, with BRITISH COLUMBIA, flanked by tiny maple leaf ornaments, curved to the top edge. CANADA and DOLLAR are curved to the bottom edge, separated by a tiny maple leaf ornament. The dates 1871 and 1971 appear to the left and right of the shield respectively, both curved to the circular shape of the coin.

111

Elizabeth II 1973

The obverse is the same as described for 1968–1986. To celebrate the centennial of Prince Edward Island's entry into Confederation, the reverse device features the P.E.I. Legislature building. CANADA DOLLAR is curved to the top edge. The dates 1873 and 1973 appear to the far left and right in the exergue immediately below the building. PRINCE / EDWARD ISLAND / ÎLE DU PRINCE / ÉDOUARD appears in four lines in the exergue so that PRINCE lies between the two dates.

Elizabeth II 1974

The obverse is the same as described for 1968–1986. To celebrate the centennial of the City of Winnipeg, the reverse device features a large 100. The city's main street, as it appeared in 1874, is depicted in the first zero and, as it appeared in 1974, in the second zero. CANADA DOLLAR is curved to the bottom edge. The word WINNIPEG appears above the device and 1874–1974 appears in the exergue.

Elizabeth II 1982

The obverse features a reduced version of the same mature effigy of the Queen to the right, draped and wearing a diamond tiara. CANADA 1982 DOLLAR is curved to the top border, flanked by tiny maple leaf ornaments and ELIZABETH II is curved to the bottom border.

To celebrate the new Canadian Constitution, the reverse device depicts the well-known painting of the Fathers of Confederation. 1867 CONFEDERATION appears in two lines above the device and CONSTITUTION 1982 appears in two lines below.

Elizabeth II 1984

The obverse is the same as described for 1982. To commemorate Jacques Cartier's landing at Gaspé in 1534 the reverse features Cartier and the cross he raised. In the background, his ship rests at anchor off shore. The legend 1534 JACQUES CARTIER 1984 appears on a ribbon along the bottom border.

AUREATE BRONZE DOLLARS
Elizabeth II 1987–1989

In 1987 the shape of the dollar was changed to eleven-sided and the composition was changed to nickel, plated with aureate bronze. The obverse shows the same mature effigy of the Queen to the right, as was introduced in 1965.

The reverse shows a loon swimming to the right on a body of water with a treed island in the background. CANADA is curved above and DOLLAR below with the date appearing in the exergue below the water.

Points of wear: The eyebrow, the hair concealing the top of the ear, the hair at the temple and forehead and the centre of the band of the tiara. The drapery over the shoulder, especially the line marking the top of the queen's gown. On the reverse, the wing and head of the loon and the water lines to the lower left of the loon. The trees on the island wear next.

Elizabeth II 1990 to date
(Excluding commemorative issues)

The obverse features a contemporary effigy of the Queen, to the right, crowned and wearing a necklace and earring. ELIZABETH II is curved to the left edge and D • G • REGINA is curved to the right.

The reverse is the same as described for 1987–1989. In 1992 the loon dollar was the same as described here except for the date, which read 1867–1992. This difference should not affect the grading descriptions.

Points of wear: The cheek, the earring and the hair covering the ear. On the reverse, the wing and head of the loon and the water lines to the lower left of the loon. The trees on the island wear next.

Elizabeth II 1992

The obverse again features the contemporary effigy of the Queen introduced in 1990.

The reverse device features three children with a Canadian flag, seated before the centre block of the Parliament Buildings. CANADA is spread to the top border and DOLLAR is spread to the bottom.

Elizabeth II 1994

The obverse is the same as described for 1992. The date is shown at the bottom of the obverse. The reverse device depicts the National War Memorial in Ottawa. CANADA and DOLLAR are curved to the top border, separated by the top of the memorial.

Elizabeth II 1995

The obverse is the same as described for 1994. The reverse device represents a portion of the Peacekeeping Monument, *The Reconciliation,* and depicts three Canadian peacekeepers atop a tank. CANADA and DOLLAR are curved to the top border, separated by a small maple leaf ornament.

BI-METALLIC TWO DOLLARS

Elizabeth II 1996 to date

The circulating two dollar coin has a circular aluminum-bronze centre, within an outer ring of nickel.

The obverse displays a reduced version of the contemporary effigy of the Queen to the right, wearing a necklace and earring. The effigy vertically fills the aluminum-bronze centre of the coin. Centred in the nickel outer ring are ELIZABETH II and D • G • REGINA, separated by a maple leaf, at the top and the date at the bottom.

On the reverse, a polar bear standing on an early summer ice floe fills the aluminum-bronze centre. The word CANADA is centred on the nickel outer ring at the top and 2 DOLLARS is centred at the bottom.

GOLD FIVE AND TEN DOLLARS

George V 1912–1914

The obverse shows a robed, crowned effigy of the King to the left, wearing the chain of the Order of the Garter fastened by a bow on the shoulder. GEORGIVS V DEI GRA: REX ET IND: IMP:

The reverse bears the shield of the arms of Canada at that time, superimposed upon two branches of maple. CANADA is curved to the top border, while the date and either FIVE DOLLARS or TEN DOLLARS appear in two lines curved to the bottom. Beaded rims.

Points of wear: The eyebrow, the band and jewels of the crown and the shoulder bow. On the reverse, which is slightly convex, the centre of the shield shows wear first. The maple leaves are also vulnerable to early wear.

FINE-12

The eyebrow is indistinct. The shoulder bow and the band of the crown and its jewels are worn. The details of the robe and chain begin to blur. On the reverse, the shield is worn over nearly its entire surface. The maple leaves show wear, those adjacent to the rim showing wear over half their area. The Rim beads begin to merge.

VERY FINE-20

The eyebrow is considerably worn. The shoulder bow, band of the crown and its jewels are clear but not sharp. On the reverse, the shield is clear but not sharp. The maple leaves adjacent to the rim are worn over a third or so of their area.

EXTREMELY FINE-40

The eyebrow is worn and there is slight wear along the band of the crown. Other details are clear and sharp. On the reverse, there is slight wear at the centre of the shield and on the maple leaves adjacent to the rim. Other details are clear and sharp.

ABOUT UNCIRCULATED-50

There is slight wear on the eyebrow and on the centre of the band of the crown. On the reverse, there is very slight wear at the centre of the shield and traces of wear on the maple leaves adjacent to the rim.

GOLD SOVEREIGNS

Edward VII 1908–1910

The Ottawa mint coined Imperial sovereigns from 1908 to 1910, with a C mint mark on the reverse above the date.

The obverse features a bare-headed effigy of the King to the right. EDWARDVS VII D: G: BRITT: OMN: REX F: D: IND: IMP:

The reverse device depicts St. George slaying the dragon. The date appears in the exergue. The obverse has rim beads and the reverse has denticles.

Points of wear: The eyebrow, ear, hair and beard. On the reverse, St. George's arm and leg, the rump of the horse and the sword are subject to wear.

FINE-12

The eyebrow is indistinct and there is little detail remaining in the hair and beard. The ear is blurred. Rim beads begin to merge. On the reverse, the entire field is worn. The rider's arm and leg and the rump of the horse are considerably worn. The sword and reins are blurred. The mint mark begins to blur.

VERY FINE-20

The eyebrow is considerably worn. The hair and beard begin to wear near the ear. On the reverse, the right arm and leg are worn but clear and the rump of the horse begins to wear. The mint mark and the border denticles are clear.

EXTREMELY FINE-40

The eyebrow is definitely worn and there is slight wear on the hair, beard and top of the ear. The rim beads are clear and sharp. On the reverse, the right arm and leg are faintly worn. The border denticles and mint mark are clear and sharp.

ABOUT UNCIRCULATED-50

There is slight wear on the eyebrow. On the reverse, there is slight wear on the right arm and leg.

George V 1911, 1913–1919

The obverse features a bare-headed effigy of the King to the left. GEORGIVS V D: G: BRITT: OMN: REX F: D: IND: IMP:

The reverse is the same as used on the issues of Edward VII. Rim beads on the obverse and denticles on the reverse.

Points of wear: The eyebrow, the hair above the ear, the beard and the outline of the ear. On the reverse, St. George's arm and leg, the rump of the horse and the sword are subject to wear.

FINE-12

The eyebrow is indistinct. There is considerable wear on the beard and on the hair above the ear. The outline of the ear is indistinct. On the reverse, the entire field is worn. The rider's arm and leg and the rump of the horse are considerably worn. The sword and reins are blurred. The mint mark begins to blur.

VERY FINE-20

The eyebrow is considerably worn. The wear on the hair spreads nearer the ear. The outline of the top of the ear is clear but not sharp. The beard is slightly worn and the rim beads are clear. On the reverse, the right arm and leg are worn but clear and the rump of the horse begins to wear. The mint mark is clear.

EXTREMELY FINE-40

There is slight wear on the eyebrow and the hair above the ear. Other details are clear and sharp. On the reverse, the right arm and leg are faintly worn. Other details are clear and sharp.

ABOUT UNCIRCULATED-50

There are traces of wear on the eyebrow. On the reverse, the right arm and leg may show slight signs of wear.

NEW BRUNSWICK—HALF CENT
Victoria 1861

The obverse features a draped laureate effigy of the Queen to the left, with the hair tied in a knot at the back. The knot is held in place with a braid and the hair at the temple passes over the ear to the knot, leaving only the ear lobe visible. The laurel wreath is tied with a ribbon, the ends of which hang down over the back of the neck. One ribbon end hangs almost straight downward and the other curves inward, overlapping the nape of the neck. The robe is embroidered with the heraldic flowers of the British Isles and is held in place with a brooch. The words HONI SO are seen at the shoulder. VICTORIA D : G : is curved to the left border and BRITT:REG : F : D : is curved to the right.

The reverse shows a crown / a short horizontal line / 1861 in three lines. within a beaded inner circle, enclosed by a wreath of roses and mayflowers. HALF CENT is curved to the top border and NEW BRUNSWICK is curved to the bottom. The wreath and inscriptions are separated from the rim beads and the beaded circle by thin circular lines.

Points of wear: The eyebrow, the ribbon end touching the neck, the hair over the ear and HONI SO. On the reverse, the crown and roses wear first. The reverses of New Brunswick half cents are convex as a rule.

ABOUT GOOD-3

All but the deepest details are gone. On the reverse, the date and legends are barely legible.

GOOD-4

The hair over the ear is worn through and the braid is invisible. Facial features are blurred. On the reverse, little or no detail remains in the crown and the wreath. Circle and rim beads are badly worn.

VERY GOOD-8

The eyebrow has been worn away. There is little detail in the hair over the ear and the knot at the back. The ribbon end touching the neck has been worn away. The braid is badly worn. The details of the drapery are worn almost off. On the reverse, the vertical lines in the cap of the crown are indistinct and the central arch is worn through. The line separating the crown from the date is faint. Circle and rim beads are blurred.

FINE-12

The eyebrow is indistinct. The strands of the hair over the ear begin to merge together. The ribbon end touching the neck is considerably worn. The braid around the knot and the details of the drapery are worn. On the reverse, the crown is considerably worn. Circle and rim beads begin to run together.

VERY FINE-20

The eyebrow is considerably worn and the hair over the ear is worn. The ribbon ends and the braid are clear. The details of the drapery are clear but not sharp. On the reverse, the crown is clear but shows some wear. Circle and rim beads are clear.

EXTREMELY FINE-40

The eyebrow is worn and there is slight wear on the hair over the ear. Other details are clear and sharp. On the reverse, there is slight wear on the crown. Other details are clear and sharp. Circle and rim beads are clear and sharp.

ABOUT UNCIRCULATED-50

There is slight wear on the eyebrow. On the reverse, there are traces of wear on the crown.

NEW BRUNSWICK—CENTS

Victoria 1861, 1864

The obverse features the draped laureate effigy of the Queen to the left, as on the New Brunswick half cent.

The reverse design is also the same as the half cent except for the legend. ONE CENT is curved to the top border and NEW BRUNSWICK is curved to the bottom.

Points of wear: The eyebrow, the ribbon end touching the neck, the hair over the ear and HONI SO. On the reverse, the crown and roses wear first. The reverses are convex.

ABOUT GOOD-3

All but the deepest details are gone. On the reverse, the date and legends are barely legible.

GOOD-4

The hair over the ear is worn through and the braid is invisible. Facial features are blurred. On the reverse, little or no detail remains in the crown and the wreath. Circle and rim beads are badly blurred.

VERY GOOD-8

The eyebrow has been worn away. There is little detail in the hair over the ear and the knot at the back. The ribbon end touching the neck has been worn away. The braid is badly worn. The details of the drapery are worn almost off. On the reverse, the vertical lines in the cap of the crown are indistinct and the central arch is worn through on convex reverses. The line separating the crown from the date is faint. Circle and rim beads are blurred.

FINE-12

The eyebrow is indistinct. The strands of the hair over the ear begin to merge together. The ribbon end touching the neck is considerably worn. The braid around the knot and the details of the drapery are worn. On convex reverses, the crown is considerably worn. On flat reverses the wreath is worn. Circle and rim beads begin to run together.

VERY FINE-20

The eyebrow is considerably worn and the hair over the ear is worn. The ribbon end and braid are clear. The details of the drapery are clear but not sharp. On the reverse, the crown is clear but shows some wear. Circle and rim beads are clear.

EXTREMELY FINE-40

The eyebrow is worn and there is slight wear on the hair over the ear. Other details are clear and sharp. On the reverse, there is slight wear on the crown or the wreath. Other details are clear and sharp. Circle and rim beads are clear and sharp.

ABOUT UNCIRCULATED-50

There is slight wear on the eyebrow. On the reverse, there are traces of wear on the crown or the wreath.

NEW BRUNSWICK–SILVER FIVE CENTS

Victoria 1862, 1864

The obverse displays an effigy of the Queen to the left, laureate, with the hair tied in a knot or chignon at the back, leaving a pendant lock of hair. The hair at the temple is braided, the braid passing around and below the ear to the knot of hair. VICTORIA D : G : REG: • with NEW BRUNSWICK below.

The reverse displays 5 CENTS and date in three lines, within a wreath of maple leaves, surmounted by St. Edward's crown. Beaded rims.

Points of wear: The eyebrow, the braid of hair below and in front of the ear, the knot of hair at the back and the leaves of the laurel wreath nearest the ear. On the reverse, wear begins on the crown and the wreath leaves immediately flanking the bow.

ABOUT GOOD-3

All but the deepest details are gone. On the reverse, the legend is badly blurred.

GOOD-4

The braid of the hair and the laurel leaves near the ear have been worn through. The knot of hair at the back is badly worn. The facial features are blurred. On the reverse, there is no detail in the wreath or crown. The legend is worn. Rim beads are indistinct.

VERY GOOD-8

The eyebrow has been worn away and no detail remains in the braid around the ear. The laurel leaves are considerably worn, those nearest the ear being almost worn through. There is little detail to the knot of hair. On the reverse, there is little detail remaining in the wreath and crown. Rim beads are blurred.

FINE-12

The eyebrow is indistinct and the segments of the braid begin to merge, those nearest the ear being considerably worn. The laurel leaves are somewhat worn, especially near the ear and the segments of the knot begin to merge. On the reverse, all the leaves are worn; the outer third or so of the top leaves and the outer half or more of the bottom ones. The pearls in the arches of the crown begin to merge. Rim beads begin to merge.

VERY FINE-20

The eyebrow is considerably worn. The segments ot the braid are clear but not sharp, those nearest the ear in some cases beginning to run together. The laurel leaves are clear, but those adjacent to the ear may be a bit blurred. On the reverse, wear extends up the sides of the wreath, the outer third or so of the bottom leaves being worn. The other details are clear.

EXTREMELY FINE-40

The eyebrow is worn. The braid is slightly worn but generally clear. The laurel leaves are clear and sharp, only those nearest the ear showing a bit of wear. Other details are clear and sharp. On the reverse, there is slight wear on the outer edges of the leaves, especially the bottom leaves. Other details are clear and sharp.

ABOUT UNCIRCULATED-50

There is slight wear on the eyebrow and parts of the braid. On the reverse, there is slight wear on the bottom leaves of the wreath.

NEW BRUNSWICK—SILVER TEN CENTS

Victoria 1862, 1864

The obverse displays an effigy of the Queen to the left, laureate, with the hair tied in a knot or chignon at the back, leaving a pendant lock of hair. The hair at the temple is braided, the braid passing around and below the ear to the knot of hair. • VICTORIA D : G : REG: • with NEW BRUNSWICK below.

The reverse displays 10 CENTS and date in three lines, within a wreath of maple leaves, surmounted by St. Edward's crown. Rim beads.

Points of wear: The eyebrow, the braid of hair below and in front of the ear; the knot of hair at the back and the leaves of the laurel wreath nearest the ear. On the reverse, wear begins on the crown and the wreath leaves immediately flanking the bow.

ABOUT GOOD-3

All but the deepest details are gone. On the reverse, the legend is badly blurred.

GOOD-4

The braid of the hair and the laurel leaves near the ear are worn through. The knot of hair at the back is badly worn. The facial features are blurred. On the reverse, there is no detail to the wreath or crown. The legend is worn. Rim beads are indistinct.

VERY GOOD-8

The eyebrow has been worn away and no detail remains in the braid around the ear. The laurel leaves are considerably worn, those nearest the ear being almost worn through. There is little detail to the knot of hair. On the reverse, there is little detail remaining in the wreath and crown. Rim beads are blurred.

FINE-12

The eyebrow is indistinct and the segments of the braid begin to merge, those nearest the ear being considerably worn. The laurel leaves are somewhat worn, especially near the ear and the segments of the knot begin to merge. On the reverse, all the leaves are worn; the outer third or so of the top leaves and the outer half or more of the bottom ones. The pearls in the arches of the crown begin to merge. Rim beads begin to merge.

VERY FINE-20

The eyebrow is considerably worn. The segments ot the braid are clear but not sharp, those nearest the ear in some cases beginning to run together. The laurel leaves are clear, but those nearest the ear may be a bit blurred. On the reverse, wear extends up the sides of the wreath, the outer third or so of the bottom leaves being worn. Other details are clear.

EXTREMELY FINE-40

The eyebrow is worn. The braid is slightly worn but generally clear. Other details are clear and sharp. The laurel leaves are clear and sharp, only those next to the ear showing a bit of wear. On the reverse, there is slight wear on the outer edges of the leaves, especially the bottom leaves. Other details are clear and sharp.

ABOUT UNCIRCULATED-50

There is slight wear on the eyebrow. On the reverse, there are traces of wear on the bottom leaves of the wreath.

NEW BRUNSWICK—SILVER TWENTY CENTS

Victoria 1862, 1864

The obverse displays an effigy of the Queen to the left, laureate, with the hair tied in a knot or chignon at the back, leaving a pendant lock of hair. The hair at the temple is braided, the braid passing around and below the ear to the knot of hair. • VICTORIA D:G: REG: • with NEW BRUNSWICK below

The reverse displays 20 CENTS and date in three lines, within a very heavy wreath of smaller maple leaves, surmounted by a large St. Edward's crown. Beaded rims.

Points of wear: The eyebrow, the braid of hair below and in front of the ear; the knot of hair at the back and the laurel leaves nearest the ear. On the reverse, wear begins on the large leaves flanking the date.

ABOUT GOOD-3

All but the deepest details are gone. On the reverse, the legend is barely legible.

GOOD-4

The braid of the hair and the laurel leaves near the ear have been worn through. The knot of hair at the back is badly worn. The facial features are blurred. On the reverse, no detail remains in the wreath and crown. The legend is blurred. Rim beads are indistinct.

VERY GOOD-8

The eyebrow has been worn away and no detail remains in the braid around the ear. The laurel leaves are considerably worn, those nearest the ear being almost worn through. There is little detail to the knot of hair. On the reverse, there is little detail remaining in the wreath. The pearls in the arches of the crown are blurred and the legend is considerably worn. Rim beads are blurred.

FINE-12

The eyebrow is indistinct and the segments of the braid begin to merge, those nearest the ear being considerably worn. The laurel leaves are somewhat worn, especially near the ear and the segments of the knot begin to merge. On the reverse, all the leaves of the wreath are worn. The pearls in the arches of the crown begin to merge. The legend begins to thicken. Rim beads begin to merge.

VERY FINE-20

The eyebrow is considerably worn. The segments of the braid are clear but not sharp, those nearest the ear in some cases beginning to run together. The laurel leaves are clear except for those nearest the ear. On the reverse, wear on the wreath extends along the sides of the leaves adjacent the legend. The crown is clear but not sharp.

EXTREMELY FINE-40

The eyebrow is worn. The braid is slightly worn but clear. The laurel leaves are clear and sharp, only those next to the ear showing a bit of wear. Other details are clear and sharp. On the reverse, there is slight wear on the edges of the large leaves flanking the date. Other details are clear and sharp.

ABOUT UNCIRCULATED-50

There is slight wear on the eyebrow and parts of the braid. On the reverse, there is slight wear on the leaves of the wreath flanking the date.

NEWFOUNDLAND—LARGE CENTS

Victoria 1865–1896

The obverse features the draped laureate effigy of the Queen to the left, with the hair tied in a knot at the back. The knot is held in place with a braid and the hair at the temple passes over the ear to the knot, leaving only the ear lobe visible. The laurel wreath is tied with a ribbon, the ends of which hang down over the back of the neck. One ribbon end hangs almost straight downward and the other curves inward, overlapping the nape of the neck. The robe is embroidered with the heraldic flowers of the British Isles and is held in place with a brooch. The words HONI SO are seen at the shoulder. VICTORIA is curved to the left border and D: G: REG: is curved to the right.

The reverse shows a crown / short horizontal line / the date, in three lines within a beaded inner circle enclosed by a wreath of pitcher plant. ONE CENT is curved to the top border and NEWFOUNDLAND is curved to the bottom. The wreath and inscriptions are separated from the rim beads and the beaded circle by thin circular lines.

Points of wear: The eyebrow, the ribbon end touching the neck, the hair over the ear and HONI SO. On the reverse, the right half of the crown wears first. Reverses are somewhat convex from 1872 to 1896.

ABOUT GOOD-3

All but the deepest details are gone. On the reverse, the date and legends are barely legible.

GOOD-4

The hair over the ear has been worn through and the braid is invisible. Facial features are blurred. On the reverse, little or no detail remains in the crown and the wreath. Circle and rim beads are badly blurred.

VERY GOOD-8

The eyebrow has been worn away. There is little detail in the hair over the ear and the knot at the back. The ribbon end touching the neck has been worn away. The braid is badly worn. The details of the drapery have been worn almost off. On the reverse, the wreath and inscriptions are considerably worn and the right side of the crown is worn through on convex reverses. Circle and rim beads are blurred.

FINE-12

The eyebrow is indistinct. The strands of the hair over the ear begin to merge together. The ribbon end touching the neck is considerably worn. The braid around the knot and the details of the drapery are worn. On the reverse, the crown is considerably worn and the leaves of the wreath show definite wear. The date begins to thicken. Circle and rim beads begin to blur.

VERY FINE-20

The eyebrow is considerably worn and the details of the drapery are clear but not sharp. The hair over the ear is worn while the braid and the ribbon ends are clear. On the reverse, wear in the cap of the crown extends to the fleur de lys at the right and the left side of the crown begins to wear. The crown's jewels and ermine band are clear but but not sharp. The wreath is clear but not sharp. Circle and rim beads are clear.

EXTREMELY FINE-40

The eyebrow is worn and there is slight wear on the hair over the ear. Other details are clear and sharp. On the reverse, there is slight wear at the top of the cap of the crown on the right side. Other details are clear and sharp. Circle and rim beads are clear and sharp.

ABOUT UNCIRCULATED-50

There is slight wear on the eyebrow. On the reverse, there are traces of wear at the top of the cap of the crown on the right side.

Edward VII 1904–1909

The obverse shows a robed, crowned effigy of the King to the right, wearing the chain of the Order of the Garter fastened by a bow on the shoulder. EDWARDVS VII DEI GRATIA REX IMPERATOR

The reverse shows a stylized Imperial State Crown / a short horizontal line / the date, in three lines, within a beaded circle enclosed by a wreath of pitcher plant. ONE CENT is curved to the top border and NEWFOUNDLAND is curved to the bottom. The wreath and inscriptions are separated from the rim beads and the beaded circle by thin circular lines. Beaded rims.

Points of wear: The eyebrow, the band of the crown, the hair at the temple, the ear, beard and shoulder bow. On the reverse, the central arch of the crown wears first. All dates are flat.

GOOD-4

The band of the crown, the shoulder bow and the outer rim of the ear are worn through. Little detail remains in the hair, beard and robe. On the reverse, the central arch of the crown is worn through. Other details are blurred. Circle and rim beads are badly blurred.

VERY GOOD-8

The eyebrow has been worn away. The band of the crown is worn through at the centre and the robe, hair and beard are considerably worn. The shoulder bow has been partly worn away. On the reverse, there is little detail to the crown, the central arch being worn almost through. The wreath is considerably worn. Circle and rim beads are blurred.

FINE-12

The eyebrow is indistinct and the band of the crown, jewels and shoulder bow are all considerably worn. The robe, hair and beard are worn. On the reverse the crown is quite worn and the wreath shows wear. Circle and rim beads begin to merge.

VERY FINE-20

The eyebrow is considerably worn. The band of the crown and the jewels are clear but not sharp. The hair, beard and robe are clear, but the shoulder bow is worn. On the reverse, the central arch of the crown shows some wear along its entire length. Other details are clear.

EXTREMELY FINE-40

The eyebrow is worn and the band of the crown is slightly worn at the centre. The shoulder bow is slightly worn while other details are clear and sharp. On the reverse, the central arch of the crown shows a spot of wear. Other details are clear and sharp.

ABOUT UNCIRCULATED-50

The eyebrow is slightly worn. On the reverse, there are traces of wear on the central arch of the crown.

George V 1913–1936

The obverse shows a robed, crowned effigy of the King to the left, wearing the chain of the Order of the Garter fastened by a bow on the shoulder. GEORGIVS V DEI GRA: REX ET IND: IMP:

The reverse shows a stylized Imperial State Crown / a short horizontal line / the date, in three lines, within a beaded circle enclosed by a wreath of pitcher plant. ONE CENT is curved to the top border and NEWFOUNDLAND is curved to the bottom. The wreath and inscriptions are separated from the rim beads and the beaded circle by thin circular lines. Beaded rims.

Points of wear: The Newfoundland cents of George V are peculiar in that the obverse is more vulnerable to early wear than that of the Canadian cent of this reign, despite the fact that the coins are flat. The band of the crown and the ear show wear much more readily on the Newfoundland cents. On the reverse, the central arch of the crown is the first place to show wear.

GOOD-4

The band of the crown is worn through and only the centre of the ear can be seen. There is very little detail to the robe and beard. On the reverse, the central arch of the crown is worn through. Other details are blurred.

VERY GOOD-8

The eyebrow has been worn away and the band of the crown is worn through at the middle. There is little detail to the crown and ear. There is little detail in the robe, beard and shoulder bow, the bow being partly worn through. On the reverse, there is little detail to the central arch of the crown and the wreath is considerably worn. Rim beads are blurred.

FINE-12

The eyebrow is indistinct and there is considerable wear extending down from the band of the crown to the ear. The shoulder bow is considerably worn. On the reverse, the central arch of the crown is considerably worn and the wreath shows wear. Circle and rim beads begin to merge.

VERY FINE-20

The eyebrow is considerably worn. Wear extends along the band of the crown and into the hair above the ear. The shoulder bow is worn. Other details are clear. On the reverse, the central arch of the crown shows wear along its entire length. Other details are clear.

EXTREMELY FINE-40

The eyebrow is worn and there is slight wear on the shoulder bow and the band of the crown. On the reverse, the crown shows a spot of wear on the central arch. All other details on both sides are clear and sharp.

ABOUT UNCIRCULATED-50

The eyebrow is slightly worn. On the reverse, there is slight wear on the central arch of the crown.

NEWFOUNDLAND—SMALL CENTS

George VI 1938–1947

The obverse displays a crowned effigy of the King to the left. GEORGIVS VI DEI GRA. REX ET IND. IMP.

The reverse shows a pitcher plant in bloom, its stem dividing the date. NEWFOUNDLAND is curved to the top border and • ONE CENT. • is curved to the bottom. Beaded rims.

Points of wear: The band of the crown, the hair at the temple and above the ear. On the reverse, the flower head is the first place to wear. The leaves on the left side of the plant wear next.

VERY GOOD-8

The band of the crown and the outline of the ear are almost worn through and little detail remains in the hair. On the reverse, the leaves and flower show little detail and the legend is thickened by wear. Rim beads are blurred.

FINE-12

The band of the crown is considerably worn. The strands of hair begin to merge and the outline of the ear loses its clarity. On the reverse, the pitcher plant is considerably worn and the legend begins to thicken. Rim beads begin to blur.

VERY FINE-20

Wear extends along the band of the crown. Other details are clear. On the reverse, the flower head and the left leaves are worn and the right leaves begin to wear. Other details are clear. Rim beads are clear.

EXTREMELY FINE-40

There is slight wear on the band of the crown. On the reverse, the flower head and the left leaves are slightly worn. Other details on both sides are clear and sharp.

ABOUT UNCIRCULATED-50

There are traces of wear at the centre of the band of the crown. On the reverse, there are traces of wear on the flower head and the leaves on the left side of the plant.

NEWFOUNDLAND—SILVER FIVE CENTS

Victoria 1865–1896

The obverse displays an effigy of the Queen to the left, laureate, with the hair tied in a knot or chignon at the back, leaving a pendant lock of hair. The hair at the temple is braided, the braid passing around and below the ear to the knot of hair at the back. VICTORIA D: G: REG: is curved to the top border and NEWFOUNDLAND is curved to the bottom.

The reverse displays 5 CENTS and the date in three lines, within a beaded circle enclosed by a cartouche or continuous ornamental frame. Beaded rims.

Points of wear: The eyebrow, the braid of hair below and in front of the ear; the knot of hair at the back and the leaves of the laurel wreath nearest the ear. On the reverse, the details of the cartouche wear first.

ABOUT GOOD-3

Only the deepest details are visible. On the reverse, the legend is barely legible.

GOOD-4

The braid of hair and the laurel leaves next to the ear are worn through and the knot of hair at the back is badly worn. Facial features are blurred. On the reverse, the legend is badly worn and the cartouche is almost worn through in places. Circle and rim beads are indistinct.

VERY GOOD-8

The eyebrow has been worn away and there is no detail to the braid around the ear. The laurel leaves are considerably worn, those nearest the ear being almost worn through. There is little detail to the knot of hair at the back. On the reverse, the legend shows wear, the N of CENTS being worn almost through on convex reverses. The cartouche begins to appear disconnected or broken. Circle and rim beads are blurred.

FINE-12

The eyebrow is indistinct and the segments of the braid begin to merge, those nearest the ear being considerably worn. The laurel leaves are somewhat worn, especially near the ear and the segments of the knot begin to merge together. On the reverse, the legend and cartouche are considerably worn, but never worn through. Circle and rim beads begin to blur.

VERY FINE-20

The eyebrow is considerably worn. The segments of the braid are clear but not sharp, those nearest the ear sometimes running together. The laurel leaves are clear except for those next to the ear. On the reverse, wear covers the whole of CENTS, especially on convex reverses. The cartouche shows wear. Circle and rim beads are clear.

EXTREMELY FINE-40

The eyebrow is worn. The braid is worn but clear. The laurel leaves are clear and sharp, only those next to the ear showing a bit of wear. Other details are clear and sharp. On the reverse, there is slight wear on the N of CENTS and on the cartouche. Circle and rim beads are clear and sharp.

ABOUT UNCIRCULATED-50

There is slight wear on the eyebrow and parts of the braid. On the reverse, there is slight wear on the N of CENTS and spots of wear along the cartouche.

Edward VII 1903–1908

The obverse shows a robed, crowned effigy of the King to the right, wearing the chain of the Order of the Garter fastened by a bow on the shoulder. EDWARDVS VII D. G. REX IMPERATOR.

The reverse shows 5 CENTS and the date in three lines within a circle opening into ornamentation at the bottom. NEWFOUNDLAND appears at the top, between the border and the circle. Beaded rims.

Points of wear: The eyebrow, band of the crown, shoulder bow, ear and beard. The reverses wear fairly evenly.

ABOUT GOOD-3

Only the deepest details are visible. On the reverse, the legend is barely legible.

GOOD-4

The band of the crown, the outer rim of the ear and the shoulder bow are worn through. There is little detail to the robe, chain, hair and beard. On the reverse, the legend is worn through in some places.

VERY GOOD-8

The eyebrow has been worn away and the band of the crown is worn through in the middle. The shoulder bow is partly worn through and little detail remains in the chain and robe. The hair and beard are considerably worn and the outline of the ear is indistinct. On the reverse, the legend is considerably thickened by wear and the bottom ornamentation is worn. Rim beads are blurred.

FINE-12

The eyebrow is indistinct while the band of the crown and the shoulder bow are considerably worn. On the reverse, the legend and bottom ornamentation are thickened by wear but by no means are they worn through anywhere. Rim beads begin to merge.

VERY FINE-20

The eyebrow is considerably worn. The band of the crown and the jewels are clear but not sharp. The shoulder bow, hair and beard are slightly worn. The details of the robe and chain are clear. On the reverse the legend is worn but clear. Rim beads are clear.

EXTREMELY FINE-40

The eyebrow is worn and there is slight wear at the band of the crown and the shoulder bow. Other details are clear and sharp. On the reverse, there is slight wear but most details are clear and sharp. Rim beads are clear and sharp.

ABOUT UNCIRCULATED-50

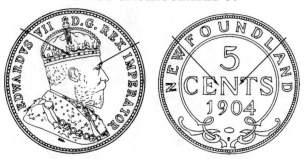

The eyebrow is slightly worn. On the reverse, there are traces of wear on the legend.

George V 1912–1929

The obverse shows a robed, crowned effigy of the King to the left, wearing the chain of the Order of the Garter fastened by a bow on the shoulder. GEORGIVS V DEI GRA: REX ET IND: IMP:

The reverse displays 5 CENTS and the date in three lines within a circle opening into ornamentation at the bottom. NEWFOUNDLAND appears at the top, between the border and the circle. Beaded rims.

Points of wear: The eyebrow, band of the crown and shoulder bow. On the reverse, wear occurs fairly evenly.

ABOUT GOOD-3

Only the deepest details are visible. On the reverse, the legend is barely legible.

GOOD-4

The band of the crown and the shoulder bow are worn through and there is little detail to the robe. On the reverse, the legend is worn through in some places.

VERY GOOD-8

The eyebrow has been worn away. The band of the crown and the jewels are considerably worn at the centre. The shoulder bow shows considerable wear and robe has little detail remaining. On the reverse, the legend is considerably thickened by wear and the bottom ornamentation is worn. Rim beads are blurred.

FINE-12

The eyebrow is indistinct. The shoulder bow, the band of the crown and the jewels are worn. The details of the robe and chain begin to blur. On the reverse, the legend and bottom ornamentation are thickened by wear, but by no means are they worn through anywhere. Rim beads begin to merge.

VERY FINE-20

The eyebrow is considerably worn. The band of the crown, jewels and shoulder bow are all clear but not sharp. On the reverse, the centre legend is worn but clear. Rim beads are clear.

EXTREMELY FINE-40

The eyebrow is worn and there is slight wear along the band of the crown. Other details are clear and sharp. On the reverse, there is slight even wear but generally clear and sharp in most places.

ABOUT UNCIRCULATED-50

There is slight wear on the eyebrow. On the reverse, there are traces of wear on the centre legend.

George VI 1938–1947

The obverse features a crowned effigy of the King to the left. GEORGIVS VI DEI GRA. REX ET IND. IMP.

The reverse shows 5 CENTS and the date in three lines within a circle opening into ornamentation at the bottom. NEWFOUNDLAND appears at the top, between the border and the circle. Beaded rims.

Points of wear: The band of the crown, the ear, and the hair at the temple and above the ear. On the reverse, the wear occurs fairly evenly.

VERY GOOD-8

The band of the crown and the outline of the ear are worn almost through and there is little detail to the hair. On the reverse, the centre legend is considerably thickened by wear and the ornamentation at the bottom is worn. Rim beads are blurred.

FINE-12

The band of the crown is considerably worn. Strands of hair begin to merge and the outline of the ear loses its clarity. On the reverse, the centre legend is thickened by wear, but never worn through. Rim beads begin to merge.

VERY FINE-20

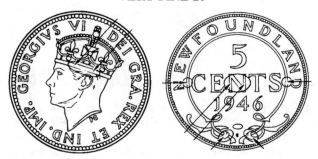

Wear extends along the band of the crown. Other details are clear. On the reverse, the centre legend is worn but clear. Rim beads are clear.

EXTREMELY FINE-40

There is slight wear on the band of the crown. On the reverse, there is slight wear on the centre legend. Other details on both sides are clear and sharp.

ABOUT UNCIRCULATED-50

There is very slight wear on the band of the crown. On the reverse, there are traces of wear on the centre legend.

NEWFOUNDLAND—SILVER TEN CENTS

Victoria 1865–1896

The obverse displays an effigy of the Queen to the left, laureate, with the hair tied in a knot or chignon at the back, leaving a pendant lock of hair. The hair at the temple is braided, the braid passing around and below the ear to the knot of hair at the back. VICTORIA D : G : REG: with • NEWFOUNDLAND below

The reverse displays 10 CENTS and the date in three lines, within a beaded circle enclosed by a cartouche or continuous ornamental frame. Beaded rims.

Points of wear: The eyebrow, the braid of hair below and in front of the ear; the knot of hair at the back and the leaves of the laurel wreath nearest the ear. On the reverse, the details of the cartouche wear first.

ABOUT GOOD-3

Only the deepest details are visible. On the reverse, the legend is barely legible.

GOOD-4

The braid of hair and the laurel leaves next to the ear are worn through and the knot of hair at the back is badly worn. Facial features are blurred. On the reverse, the centre legend is badly worn and the cartouche is almost worn through in places. Circle and rim beads are indistinct.

VERY GOOD-8

The eyebrow has been worn away and there is no detail to the braid around the ear. The laurel leaves are considerably worn, those nearest the ear being almost worn through. There is little detail to the knot of hair at the back. On the reverse, the centre legend shows wear, the N of CENTS being worn almost through on convex reverses. The cartouche begins to appear disconnected or broken. Circle and rim beads are blurred.

FINE-12

The eyebrow is indistinct and the segments of the braid begin to merge, those nearest the ear being considerably worn. The laurel leaves are somewhat worn, especially near the ear and the segments of the knot begin to merge. On the reverse, the centre legend and cartouche are definitely worn, but never worn through. Circle and rim beads begin to blur.

VERY FINE-20

The eyebrow is considerably worn. The segments of the braid are clear but not sharp, those nearest the ear sometimes running together. The laurel leaves are clear except for those nearest the ear. On the reverse, wear covers the whole of CENTS, especially on convex reverses. The cartouche shows wear. Circle and rim beads are clear.

EXTREMELY FINE-40

The eyebrow is worn. The braid is worn but clear. The laurel leaves are clear and sharp, only those nearest the ear showing a bit of wear. Other details are clear and sharp. On the reverse, there is slight wear on the N of CENTS and on the cartouche. Circle and rim beads are clear and sharp.

ABOUT UNCIRCULATED-50

There is slight wear on the eyebrow and parts of the braid. On the reverse, there is slight wear on the N of CENTS.

Edward VII 1903, 1904

The obverse features a robed, crowned effigy of the King to the right, wearing the chain of the Order of the Garter fastened by a bow on the shoulder. EDWARDVS VII D. G. REX IMPERATOR

The reverse shows 10 CENTS and the date in three lines within a circle opening into ornamentation at the bottom. NEWFOUNDLAND appears at the top, between the border and the circle. Beaded rims.

Points of wear: The eyebrow, band of the crown, shoulder bow, ear and beard. The reverse wears fairly evenly.

ABOUT GOOD-3

Only the deepest details are visible. On the reverse, the legend is barely legible.

GOOD-4

The band of the crown, the outer rim of the ear and the shoulder bow are worn through. There is little detail to the robe, chain, hair and beard. On the reverse, the centre legend is worn through in some places.

VERY GOOD-8

The eyebrow has worn away and the band of the crown is worn through in the middle. The shoulder bow is worn partly through and little detail remains in the chain and robe. The hair and beard are considerably worn and the outline of the ear is indistinct. On the reverse, the centre legend is considerably thickened by wear and the bottom ornamentation is worn. Rim beads are blurred.

FINE-12

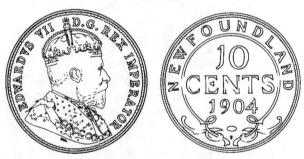

The eyebrow is indistinct while the band of the crown and the shoulder bow are considerably worn. On the reverse, the centre legend and bottom ornamentation are thickened by wear but by no means are they worn through anywhere. Rim beads begin to merge.

VERY FINE-20

The eyebrow is considerably worn. The band of the crown and the jewels are clear but not sharp. The shoulder bow, hair and beard are slightly worn. The details of the robe and chain are clear. On the reverse the centre legend is worn but clear. Rim beads are clear.

EXTREMELY FINE-40

The eyebrow is worn and there is slight wear at the band of the crown and shoulder bow. Other details are clear and sharp. On the reverse, there is slight wear but most details are clear and sharp. Rim beads are clear and sharp.

ABOUT UNCIRCULATED-50

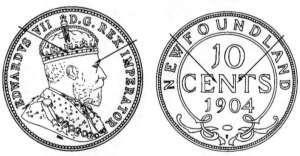

The eyebrow and band of the crown are slightly worn. On the reverse, there are traces of wear on the centre legend.

George V 1912–1919

The obverse shows a robed, crowned effigy of the King to the left, wearing the chain of the Order of the Garter fastened by a bow on the shoulder. GEORGIVS V DEI GRA: REX ET IND: IMP :

The reverse displays 10 CENTS and the date in three lines within a circle opening into ornamentation at the bottom. NEWFOUNDLAND appears at the top, between the border and the circle. Beaded rims.

Points of wear: The eyebrow, band of the crown and shoulder bow. On the reverse, wear occurs fairly evenly.

ABOUT GOOD-3

Only the deepest details are visible. On the reverse, the legend is barely legible.

GOOD-4

The band of the crown and the shoulder bow are worn through and there is little detail to the robe. On the reverse, the centre legend is worn through in some places.

VERY GOOD-8

The eyebrow has been worn away. The band of the crown and the jewels are worn through at the centre. The shoulder bow shows considerable wear and robe has little detail remaining. On the reverse, the centre legend is considerably thickened by wear and the bottom ornamentation is worn. Rim beads are blurred.

FINE-12

The eyebrow is indistinct. The shoulder bow, the band of the crown and the jewels are worn. The details of the robe and chain begin to blur. On the reverse, the centre legend and bottom ornamentation are thickened by wear, but by no means are they worn through anywhere. Rim beads begin to merge.

VERY FINE-20

The eyebrow is considerably worn. The band of the crown, jewels and shoulder bow are all clear but not sharp. On the reverse, the centre legend is worn but clear. Rim beads are clear.

EXTREMELY FINE-40

The eyebrow is worn and there is slight wear along the band of the crown. Other details are clear and sharp. On the reverse, there is slight even wear but generally clear and sharp in most places.

ABOUT UNCIRCULATED-50

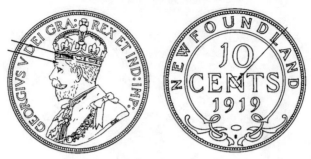

There is slight wear on the eyebrow. On the reverse, traces of wear are visible on the legend.

George VI 1938–1947

The obverse features a crowned effigy of the King to the left. The effigy is truncated at the base of the neck. GEORGIVS VI DEI GRA. REX ET IND. IMP.

The reverse shows 10 CENTS and the date in three lines within a circle opening into ornamentation at the bottom. NEWFOUNDLAND appears at the top, between the border and the circle. Beaded rims.

Points of wear: The band of the crown, the ear and the hair at the temple and above the ear. On the reverse, the wear occurs fairly evenly.

VERY GOOD-8

The band of the crown and the outline of the ear are worn almost through and there is little detail to the hair. On the reverse, the centre legend is considerably thickened by wear and the ornamentation at the bottom is worn. Rim beads are blurred.

FINE-12

The band of the crown is considerably worn. The outline of the ear loses its clarity and the strands of hair begin to merge. On the reverse, the centre legend is thickened by wear, but never worn through. Rim beads begin to merge.

VERY FINE-20

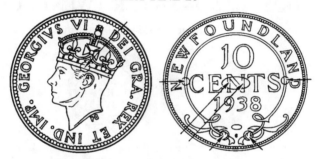

Wear extends along the band of the crown. Other details are clear. On the reverse, the centre legend is worn but clear. Rim beads are clear.

EXTREMELY FINE-40

There is slight wear on the band of the crown. On the reverse, there is slight wear on the centre legend. Other details on both sides are clear and sharp.

ABOUT UNCIRCULATED-50

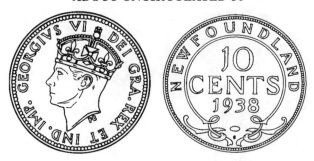

There is very slight wear at the centre of the band of the crown. On the reverse, there are traces of wear on the centre legend.

NEWFOUNDLAND—SILVER TWENTY CENTS

Victoria 1865–1900

The obverse displays an effigy of the Queen to the left, laureate, with the hair tied in a knot or chignon at the back, leaving a pendant lock of hair. The hair at the temple is braided, the braid passing around and below the ear to the knot of hair at the back. VICTORIA D: G: REG: with • NEWFOUNDLAND • below.

The reverse displays 20 CENTS and the date in three lines, within a beaded circle enclosed by a cartouche or continuous ornamental frame. Beaded rims.

Points of wear: The eyebrow, the braid of hair below and in front of the ear; the knot of hair at the back and the leaves of the laurel wreath nearest the ear. On the reverse, the details of the cartouche wear first. Reverses are convex in 1873 and 1876.

ABOUT GOOD-3

Only the deepest details are visible. On the reverse, the legend is barely legible.

GOOD-4

The braid of hair and the laurel leaves nearest the ear are worn through and the knot of hair at the back is badly worn. Facial features are blurred. On the reverse, the legend is badly worn and the cartouche is almost worn through in places. Circle and rim beads are indistinct.

164

VERY GOOD-8

The eyebrow has been worn away and there is no detail to the braid around the ear. The laurel leaves are considerably worn, those nearest the ear being worn almost through. There is little detail to the knot of hair at the back. On the reverse, the legend shows wear, the N of CENTS being worn almost through on convex reverses. The cartouche begins to appear disconnected or broken. Circle and rim beads are blurred.

FINE-12

The eyebrow is indistinct and the segments of the braid begin to merge, those nearest the ear being considerably worn. The laurel leaves are somewhat worn, especially those nearest the ear and the segments of the knot begin to merge. On the reverse, the legend and cartouche are considerably worn, but never worn through. Circle and rim beads begin to blur.

VERY FINE-20

The eyebrow is considerably worn. The segments of the braid are clear but not sharp, those nearest the ear sometimes running together. The laurel leaves are clear except for those nearest the ear. On the reverse, wear covers the whole of CENTS, especially on convex reverses. The cartouche shows wear. Circle and rim beads are clear.

EXTREMELY FINE-40

The eyebrow is worn. The braid is worn but clear. The laurel leaves are clear and sharp, only those nearest the ear showing a bit of wear. Other details are clear and sharp. On the reverse, there is slight wear on the N of CENTS and on the cartouche. Circle and rim beads are clear and sharp.

ABOUT UNCIRCULATED-50

There is slight wear on the eyebrow and parts of the braid. On the reverse, there are traces of wear on the N of CENTS.

Edward VII 1904

The obverse shows a robed, crowned effigy of the King to the right, wearing the chain of the Order of the Garter fastened by a bow on the shoulder. EDWARDVS VII DEI GRATIA REX IMPERATOR The obverse is markedly convex.

The reverse legend 20 CENTS 1904 appears in three lines within a circle opening into ornamentation at the bottom. NEWFOUNDLAND appears at the top, between the border and the circle. Beaded rims.

Points of wear: The eyebrow, band of the crown, shoulder bow, ear and beard. On the reverse, the ornamentation at the bottom is first to wear. The wear then spreads into the centre legend.

ABOUT GOOD-3

Only the deepest details are visible. On the reverse, the legend is barely legible.

GOOD-4

The band of the crown, the outer rim of the ear and the shoulder bow are worn through. There is little detail to the robe, chain, hair and beard. On the reverse, the legends are considerably worn. The bottom ornamentation is badly worn.

VERY GOOD-8

The eyebrow has been worn away and the band of the crown is worn through in the middle. The shoulder bow is worn partly through and little detail remains in the chain and robe. The hair and beard are considerably worn and the outline of the ear is indistinct. On the reverse, the legend is considerably thickened by wear and the bottom ornamentation is worn. Rim beads are blurred.

FINE-12

The eyebrow is indistinct while the band of the crown and the shoulder bow are considerably worn. On the reverse, the centre legend and bottom ornamentation are thickened by wear but by no means are they worn through anywhere. Rim beads begin to merge.

VERY FINE-20

The eyebrow is considerably worn. The band of the crown and the jewels are clear but not sharp. The shoulder bow, hair and beard are slightly worn. The details of the robe and chain are clear. On the reverse the centre legend is worn but clear. Rim beads are clear.

EXTREMELY FINE-40

The eyebrow is worn and there is slight wear at the band of the crown and shoulder bow. Other details are clear and sharp. On the reverse, there is slight wear but most details are clear and sharp. Rim beads are clear and sharp.

ABOUT UNCIRCULATED-50

The eyebrow and the band of the crown in the centre are slightly worn. On the reverse, there are traces of wear on the N of CENTS and on the ornamentation.

George V 1912

The obverse shows a robed, crowned effigy of the King to the left, wearing the chain of the Order of the Garter fastened by a bow on the shoulder. GEORGIVS V DEI GRA: REX ET IND: IMP:

The reverse displays 20 CENTS 1912 in three lines within a circle opening into an ornamentation at the bottom. NEWFOUNDLAND appears at the top, between the border and the circle. Beaded rims.

Points of wear: The eyebrow, band of the crown and shoulder bow. On the reverse, wear occurs fairly evenly.

ABOUT GOOD-3

Only the deepest details are visible. On the reverse, the legend is barely legible.

GOOD-4

The band of the crown and the shoulder bow are worn through and there is little detail to the robe. On the reverse, the centre legend is worn through in some places.

VERY GOOD-8

The eyebrow has been worn away. The band of the crown and the jewels are worn through at the centre. The shoulder bow shows considerable wear and the robe has little detail remaining. On the reverse, the legend is considerably thickened by wear and the bottom ornamentation is worn. Rim beads are blurred.

FINE-12

The eyebrow is indistinct. The shoulder bow, the band of the crown and the jewels are worn. The details of the robe and chain begin to blur. On the reverse, the centre legend and bottom ornamentation are thickened by wear, but by no means are they worn through anywhere. Rim beads begin to merge.

VERY FINE-20

The eyebrow is considerably worn. The band of the crown, jewels and shoulder bow are all clear but not sharp. On the reverse, the centre legend is worn but clear. Rim beads are clear.

EXTREMELY FINE-40

The eyebrow is worn and there is slight wear along the band of the crown. Other details are clear and sharp. On the reverse, there is slight even wear but details are generally clear and sharp in most places.

ABOUT UNCIRCULATED-50

There is slight wear on the eyebrow. On the reverse, there are traces of wear on the N of CENTS.

NEWFOUNDLAND—SILVER TWENTY-FIVE CENTS

George V 1917, 1919

The obverse shows a robed, crowned effigy of the King to the left, wearing the chain of the Order of the Garter fastened by a bow on the shoulder. GEORGIVS V DEI GRA: REX ET IND: IMP:

The reverse displays 25 CENTS and the date in three lines within a circle opening into ornamentation at the bottom. NEWFOUNDLAND appears at the top, between the border and the circle. Beaded rims.

Points of wear: The eyebrow, band of the crown and shoulder bow. The reverse, being convex, wears first at the N of CENTS.

ABOUT GOOD-3

Only the deepest details are visible. On the reverse, the legend is barely legible.

GOOD-4

The band of the crown and the shoulder bow are worn through and there is little detail to the robe. On the reverse, the legend is worn through at the centre.

VERY GOOD-8

The eyebrow has worn away. The band of the crown and the jewels are worn through at the centre. The shoulder bow shows considerable wear, while the chain and robe have little detail remaining. On the reverse, the word CENTS is badly worn, often worn through at the N. Rim beads are blurred.

FINE-12

The eyebrow is indistinct. The shoulder bow, the band of the crown and the jewels are worn. The details of the robe and chain begin to blur. On the reverse, the legend is considerably thickened by wear, especially the word CENTS. Rim beads begin to merge.

VERY FINE-20

The eyebrow is considerably worn. The band of the crown, jewels and shoulder bow are all clear but not sharp. On the reverse, the word CENTS is thickened by wear. Other details are worn but clear. Rim beads are clear.

EXTREMELY FINE-40

The eyebrow is worn. There is slight wear along the band of the crown. Other details are clear and sharp. On the reverse, the N of CENTS is slightly worn. Other details are clear and sharp.

ABOUT UNCIRCULATED-50

There is slight wear on the eyebrow. On the reverse, there is slight wear on the N of CENTS.

NEWFOUNDLAND—SILVER FIFTY CENTS

Victoria 1870–1900

The obverse displays an effigy of the Queen to the left, laureate, with the hair tied in a knot or chignon at the back. The hair at the temple is braided, the braid passing around and below the ear to the knot of hair at the back. The laurel wreath is tied with a ribbon, the ends of which hang down at the back of the neck without touching it. VICTORIA DEI GRATIA REGINA with NEWFOUNDLAND below.

The reverse displays 50 CENTS and the date in three lines, within a beaded circle enclosed by a cartouche or continuous ornamental frame. Beaded rims. The reverse is generally convex from 1870 to 1888 and concave from 1894 to 1900.

Points of wear: The eyebrow, the braid of hair around the ear; the knot of hair at the back and the leaves of the laurel wreath nearest the ear. On the reverse, if convex, the N of CENTS will wear first; otherwise the details of the cartouche wear first.

ABOUT GOOD-3

Only the deepest details are visible. On the reverse, the legend is barely legible.

GOOD-4

The braid of hair and the laurel leaves next to the ear are worn through. Little of these remains on convex obverses. The knot of hair at the back is badly worn and facial features are blurred. On a convex reverse, the centre legend is badly worn, CENTS often being worn through. On a concave reverse, the cartouche is similary badly worn. Circle and rim beads are indistinct.

VERY GOOD-8

The eyebrow has been worn away and there is no detail to the braid around the ear. The laurel leaves are considerably worn, those nearest the ear being worn almost through. There is little detail to the knot of hair at the back. On a convex reverse, the centre legend begins to wear through at the N of CENTS. On a concave reverse, the cartouche begins to appear disconnected or broken. Circle and rim beads are blurred.

FINE-12

The eyebrow is indistinct and the segments of the braid begin to merge, those nearest the ear being considerably worn. The laurel leaves are somewhat worn, especially near the ear and the segments of the knot begin to merge. On the reverse, the legend or the cartouche, depending on the date of issue, will be considerably worn, but by no means will either ever be worn through. Circle and rim beads begin to merge.

VERY FINE-20

The eyebrow is considerably worn. The segments ot the braid are clear but not sharp, those nearest the ear sometimes running together. The laurel leaves are clear except for those nearest the ear. On a convex reverse, wear covers the whole of CENTS. On a concave reverse, the edge of the cartouche shows wear. Circle and rim beads are clear.

EXTREMELY FINE-40

The eyebrow is worn. The braid below the ear is worn but clear. Other details are clear and sharp. On the reverse, there is slight wear on the N of CENTS or on the cartouche. Other details are clear and sharp. Circle and rim beads are clear and sharp.

ABOUT UNCIRCULATED-50

There is slight wear on the eyebrow and parts of the braid. On the reverse, there are traces of wear on the N of CENTS or on the cartouche.

Edward VII 1904–1909

The obverse shows a robed, crowned effigy of the King to the right, wearing the chain of the Order of the Garter fastened by a bow on the shoulder. EDWARDVS VII DEI GRATIA REX IMPERATOR.

The reverse shows 50 CENTS and the date in three lines within a circle opening into ornamentation at the bottom. NEWFOUNDLAND appears at the top, between the border and the circle. Beaded rims.

Points of wear: The eyebrow, band of the crown, shoulder bow, ear and beard. On the reverse, the wear occurs evenly, since all dates are flat.

ABOUT GOOD-3

Only the deepest details are visible. On the reverse, the legend is often barely legible.

GOOD-4

The band of the crown, the outer rim of the ear and the shoulder bow are worn through. There is little detail to the robe, chain, hair and beard. On the reverse, the centre legend and the bottom ornamentation are considerably worn. Rim beads are indistinct.

VERY GOOD-8

The eyebrow has been worn away and the band of the crown is worn through in the middle. The shoulder bow is worn partly through and little detail remains in the chain and robe. Hair and beard are considerably worn. The outline of the ear is indistinct. On the reverse, the centre legend is thickened by wear and the bottom ornamentation is worn. Rim beads are blurred.

FINE-12

The eyebrow is indistinct and the band of the crown is considerably worn, but not worn through. The shoulder bow is considerably worn. On the reverse, the centre legend and bottom ornamentation are thickened by wear but by no means are they worn through anywhere. Rim beads begin to merge.

VERY FINE-20

The eyebrow is considerably worn. The band of the crown and the jewels are clear but not sharp. The shoulder bow, hair and beard are slightly worn. The details of the robe and chain are clear. On the reverse the centre legend is worn but clear. Rim beads are clear.

EXTREMELY FINE-40

The eyebrow is worn and there is slight wear at the band of the crown. Other details are clear and sharp. On the reverse, there is slight wear but most details are clear and sharp. Rim beads are clear and sharp.

ABOUT UNCIRCULATED-50

The eyebrow and the centre of the band of the crown are slightly worn. On the reverse, there are traces of wear on the N of CENTS and on the ornamentation.

George V 1911–1919

The obverse shows a robed, crowned effigy of the King to the left, wearing the chain of the Order of the Garter fastened by a bow on the shoulder. GEORGIVS V DEI GRA: REX ET IND: IMP:

The reverse displays 50 CENTS and the date in three lines within a circle opening into ornamentation at the bottom. NEWFOUNDLAND appears at the top, between the border and the circle. Beaded rims. All coins are flat.

Points of wear: The eyebrow, band of the crown and shoulder bow. The reverse wears fairly evenly over the entire surface.

ABOUT GOOD-3

Only the deepest details are visible. On the reverse, the legend is barely legible.

GOOD-4

The band of the crown and the shoulder bow are worn through and there is little detail to the robe. On the reverse, the legend is worn through in places.

VERY GOOD-8

The eyebrow has been worn away. The band of the crown and the jewels are worn through at the centre. The shoulder bow shows considerable wear, while the chain and robe have little detail remaining. On the reverse, the legend is considerably thickened by wear. The bottom ornamentation is worn. Rim beads are blurred.

FINE-12

The eyebrow is indistinct. The shoulder bow, band of the crown and jewels are worn. The details of the robe and chain begin to blur. On the reverse, the legend is considerably thickened by wear, but never worn through. Rim beads begin to blur.

VERY FINE-20

The eyebrow is considerably worn. The band of the crown, jewels and shoulder bow are all clear but not sharp. On the reverse, the centre legend is worn but clear.

EXTREMELY FINE-40

The eyebrow is worn and there is slight wear along the band of the crown. Other details are clear and sharp. On the reverse, there is slight wear overall but the details are generally clear and sharp.

ABOUT UNCIRCULATED-50

There is slight wear on the eyebrow. On the reverse, there is very slight wear on the centre legend.

NEWFOUNDLAND—GOLD TWO DOLLARS

Victoria 1865–1888

The obverse displays an effigy of the Queen to the left, laureate, with the hair tied in a knot or chignon at the back, leaving a pendant lock of hair. The hair at the temple is braided, the braid passing around and below the ear to the knot of hair at the back. VICTORIA D: G: REG: with • NEWFOUNDLAND below.

The reverse displays 2 DOLLARS and the date in three lines, within a beaded circle. Between the beaded circle and the rim beads the inscription reads TWO HUNDRED CENTS at the top and ONE HUNDRED PENCE at the bottom, separated by bi-lobed ornamentation at the left and right. Beaded rims.

Points of wear: The eyebrow, the braid of hair around the ear; the knot of hair at the back and the laurel leaves nearest the ear. On the reverse, the centre legend wears first, then the side ornaments. Some reverses are slightly convex.

VERY GOOD-8

The eyebrow has been worn away and there is no detail to the braid around the ear. The laurel leaves are considerably worn, those nearest the ear being worn almost through. There is little detail to the knot of hair at the back. On the reverse, the centre legend and the side ornaments are considerably worn. Circle and rim beads are blurred.

FINE-12

The eyebrow is indistinct and the segments of the braid begin to merge, those nearest the ear being considerably worn. The laurel leaves are worn, especially those nearest the ear and the segments of the knot begin to merge. On the reverse, the centre legend begins to thicken and the side ornaments begin to show wear. Circle and rim beads begin to blur.

VERY FINE-20

The eyebrow is considerably worn. The segments of the braid are clear but not sharp, those nearest the ear sometimes running together. The laurel leaves are clear except for those next to the ear. On the reverse, wear covers the whole of DOLLARS. The side ornaments are clear Circle and rim beads are clear.

EXTREMELY FINE-40

The eyebrow is worn. The braid is worn but clear. The laurel leaves are clear and sharp, only those nearest to the ear showing a bit of wear. Other details are clear and sharp. On the reverse, there is slight wear on the LLA of DOLLARS. Other details are clear and sharp. Circle and rim beads are clear and sharp.

ABOUT UNCIRCULATED-50

There is slight wear on the eyebrow and parts of the braid. On the reverse, there are traces of wear on the LLA of DOLLARS.

NOVA SCOTIA—HALF CENTS

Victoria 1861, 1864

The obverse features a draped laureate effigy of the Queen to the left, with the hair tied in a knot at the back. The knot is held in place with a braid and the hair at the temple passes over the ear to the knot, leaving only the ear lobe visible. The laurel wreath is tied with a ribbon, the ends of which hang down over the back of the neck. One ribbon end hangs almost straight downward and the other curves inward, overlapping the nape of the neck. The robe is embroidered with the heraldic flowers of the British Isles and is held in place with a brooch. The words HONI SO are seen at the shoulder. VICTORIA D: G: is curved to the left border and BRITT : REG : F : D: is curved to the right.

The reverse shows a crown / a short horizontal line / the date in three lines, within a beaded inner circle, enclosed by a wreath of roses and mayflowers. HALF CENT is curved to the top border and NOVA SCOTIA is curved to the bottom. The wreath and inscriptions are separated from the rim beads and the beaded circle by thin circular lines. Beaded rims.

Points of wear: The eyebrow, the ribbon end touching the neck, the hair over the ear and HONI SO. On the reverse, the crown and roses wear first.

ABOUT GOOD-3

All but the deepest details are gone. On the reverse, the legend is barely legible.

GOOD-4

The hair over the ear is worn through and the braid is invisible. Facial features are blurred. On the reverse, little or no detail remains in the crown and the wreath. Circle and rim beads are badly worn.

VERY GOOD-8

The eyebrow and the ribbon end touching the neck have been worn away. There is little detail in the hair over the ear and the knot at the back. The details of the drapery are worn almost off. The braid is badly worn. On the reverse, the vertical lines in the cap of the crown are indistinct and the central arch is worn. The line separating the crown from the date is faint. Circle and rim beads are blurred.

FINE-12

The eyebrow is indistinct. The strands of the hair over the ear begin to merge. The ribbon end touching the neck is considerably worn. The details of the drapery and the braid around the knot are worn. On the reverse, the wreath is considerably worn. Circle and rim beads begin to run together.

VERY FINE-20

The eyebrow is considerably worn. The hair over the ear is worn. The braid and the ribbon end touching the neck are clear. The details of the drapery are clear but not sharp. On the reverse, the wreath is clear but shows some wear. Circle and rim beads are clear.

EXTREMELY FINE-40

The eyebrow is worn and there is slight wear on the hair over the ear. Other details are clear and sharp. On the reverse, there is slight wear on the wreath. Other details are clear and sharp. Circle and rim beads are clear and sharp.

ABOUT UNCIRCULATED-50

There is slight wear on the eyebrow. On the reverse, there are traces of wear on the wreath.

NOVA SCOTIA—CENTS

Victoria 1861, 1862, 1864

The obverse features the same draped, laureate effigy of the Queen to the left as used on the half cents, with the hair tied in a knot at the back.

The reverse shows a crown / a short horizontal line / the date, in three lines within a beaded inner circle, enclosed by a wreath of roses and mayflowers. ONE CENT is curved to the top border and NOVA SCOTIA is curved to the bottom. The wreath and inscriptions are separated from the rim beads and the beaded circle by thin circular lines. Beaded rims.

Points of wear: The eyebrow, the ribbon end touching the neck, the hair over the ear and HONI SO. On the reverse, the crown and roses wear first. The earliest cents of 1861 have convex reverses.

ABOUT GOOD-3

All but the deepest details are gone. On the reverse, the legend is barely legible.

GOOD-4

The hair over the ear is worn through and the braid is invisible. Facial features are blurred. On the reverse, little or no detail remains in the crown and the wreath. Circle and rim beads are badly worn.

VERY GOOD-8

The eyebrow has been worn away. There is little detail in the hair over the ear and the knot at the back The ribbon end touching the neck has been worn away. The braid is badly worn. The details of the drapery are worn almost off. On the reverse, the vertical lines in the cap of the crown are indistinct and the central arch is worn, being worn through on convex reverses. The line separating the crown from the date is faint. Circle and rim beads are blurred.

FINE-12

The eyebrow is indistinct. The strands of the hair over the ear begin to merge together. The ribbon end touching the neck is considerably worn. The braid around the knot is worn. On the reverse, the wreath is considerably worn on flat reverses and the crown is considerably worn on convex reverses. Circle and rim beads begin to run together.

VERY FINE-20

The eyebrow is considerably worn and the hair over the ear is worn. The ribbon end touching the neck and braid are clear. The details of the drapery are clear but not sharp. On the reverse, the crown and wreath are clear but show some wear. Circle and rim beads are clear.

EXTREMELY FINE-40

The eyebrow is worn and there is slight wear on the hair over the ear. Other details are clear and sharp. On the reverse, there is slight wear on the wreath. Other details are clear and sharp. Circle and rim beads are clear and sharp.

The cents of 1862 are peculiar in that the obverse is generally in poorer condition than the reverse, despite the fact that the coins are flat. Either the obverse die was not struck up to the same extent as in other years or the rim was not high enough to protect the coin from wear.

ABOUT UNCIRCULATED-50

There is slight wear on the eyebrow. On the reverse, there are traces of wear on the wreath.

PRINCE EDWARD ISLAND—ONE CENT

Victoria 1871

The obverse shows a diademed effigy of the Queen to the left, within a beaded circle. The hair is tied in a knot or chignon at the back and bound with an ornamental hair band. The hair at the temple is brushed back over the ear and diadem to the knot at the back. Only the ear lobe is visible. Two ribbon ends hang down from the back, one turning outward and the other inward, overlapping the neck. VICTORIA QUEEN with • 1871 • below.

The reverse depicts the Government Seal of the colony. The device shows a large oak tree sheltering three oak saplings. The Latin phrase PARVA SUB INGENTI appears in the exergue, all within a beaded circle. Between the circle and the beeded rim appears the legend PRINCE EDWARD ISLAND above with • ONE CENT • below. Beaded rims.

Points of wear: The eyebrow, the hair over the ear, the knot at the back (especially the bottom half), the jewels of the diadem, the details of the hair band and the end of the ribbon touching the neck. On the reverse, which is generally convex, the trunk of the large oak is vulnerable to early wear.

ABOUT GOOD-3

Only the deepest details are visible. On the reverse, the trees show no detail and the legends are worn.

GOOD-4

The hair over the ear is worn through and there is no detail to the knot of hair except the division between the two halves. Only part of the band of the diadem shows any detail. The facial features are blurred and the legend shows wear. On the reverse, there is little detail in the trees and ground. The Latin motto begins to blur. Circle and rim beads are blurred.

VERY GOOD-8

The eyebrow and the ribbon end touching the neck have been worn away and little or no detail remains in the hair over the ear and the bottom half of the knot at the back. The diadem is considerably worn, with some jewels partly worn away. The hair band is worn. On the reverse, the trunk of the large oak is almost worn through on the left edge and the foliage on the lowest left branch is faint. There is little detail to the ground and the Latin motto is coarsened by wear. Circle and rim beads are somewhat blurred.

FINE-12

The eyebrow is worn almost through. The hair over the ear is worn, the strands beginning to run together. The bottom half of the knot is worn but the hair band is clear. The band of the diadem is clear but the jewels are worn. The ribbon end touching the neck is indistinct. On the reverse, the trees are considerably worn and wear extends to the ground. The Latin motto begins to thicken and the legends on both sides begin to blur.

VERY FINE-20

The eyebrow is considerably worn, while the knot of hair at the back is clear but not sharp. The hair over the ear and the jewels of the diadem are clear but not sharp. The ribbon end touching the neck is worn but the hair band is clear and sharp. On the reverse, the wear extends into the foliage of the large oak and the saplings, but details are still clear.

EXTREMELY FINE-40

The eyebrow is worn but the ribbon end touching the neck is clear. Other details are clear and sharp. On the reverse, the trunk of the large oak shows a spot of wear but other details are clear and sharp.

ABOUT UNCIRCULATED-50

There is very slight wear on the eyebrow and on the trunk of the large oak on the reverse.